GLORIA'S MIRACLE

GLORIA'S
MIRACLE

A young girl, a deadly disease and an
enduring lesson about the power of faith

BY JERRY BREWER

SAN JUAN PUBLISHING
P.O. Box 923
Woodinville, WA 98072
425-485-2813
sanjuanbooks@yahoo.com
www.sanjuanbooks.com

© 2009 by Jerry Brewer

Publisher: Michael D. McCloskey
Cover Design: Chris Rukan
Interior Design and Production: Jennifer Shontz, Red Shoe Design
Editor: Holly Wyrwich
Proofreaders: Sherrill Carlson and Shannon Hendricks

Cover photographs: *Gloria* © Paul Dudley; *Rosary* © Chris Rukan
Back cover photograph © Paul Dudley
Frontispiece: *Gloria blows kisses at the beach during summer 2007.*
    © Paul Dudley
Copyrighted photos by *The Seattle Times* used by permission
Strauss family photos used by permission

Library of Congress Control Number: 2009932253
ISBN-13: 978-0-9707399-7-1
ISBN-10: 0-9707399-7-4

First Printing 2009
10 9 8 7 6 5 4 3 2 1
Printed in United States of America

CONTENTS

For all the little angels who
sprinkle glitter on our lives

PART I

GLOW

Gloria at age one. Photo courtesy of the Strauss family

CHAPTER ONE

WHEN I HEAL HER...

The girl lay before them, feeble and flustered, seven years old and wondering about death. Soreness clogged her throat. Fatigue closed her eyes, her big, blue eyes—eyes that inspired the nickname Tweety Bird. Blood filled a suction tube every time it entered her mouth.

She was bald—all of her precious blond hair gone. She vomited a little, the only evidence her insides hadn't turned into the Mojave. Her skin felt torturously hot, the burn of a fever. Chemotherapy had blasted her body to the brink of nil.

"Gloria?" her father asked, trembling. "Have you had quality of life?"

Doug Strauss didn't expect an answer, but he had to wonder anyway. The previous night, while on his knees, he begged for perspective. *God, help me understand this. Why is my child suffering so much? God, PLEASE help me understand this!* And near the end of his plea, the words *quality of life* drifted faintly into his mind.

He thought he was being directed to explore whether his daughter had enjoyed her short time. He figured she might say she needed to go to Disneyland again, or ride a horse, or do whatever else children consider a happy life. Instead, the seven-year-old became his teacher.

"Yes, Daddy," Gloria replied in a sweet, soft tone. "Look at how many people are praying to God because of me. Even Grandpa prays the rosary now. Yeah, I've had quality of life."

Gloria understood the potential of her suffering. For six months, she had observed family and friends cloaking her in prayer, yearning to extend her life. Even people who thought of church as an annoying obligation talked to God about her.

Now, in the scariest moments of her young life, as doctors drained her body to perform a risky stem-cell transplant, she worried about her many supporters. Little Gloria Strauss hadn't lived enough to fear her own demise. She could only comprehend that it would leave people disappointed, heartbroken and confused.

So, hours before the procedure, on September 11, 2003, she confided in her mother. The family gathered around her hospital bed to pray over her stem cells, hoping they would infuse health into her worn, frail body. Gloria wept. Her mother asked, why the tears?

"Are you afraid?" Kristen Strauss wondered.

"I'm afraid I might die, not because I'm afraid of dying, but people are praying for me," Gloria told her mother.

Kristen had no response. Her daughter's perspective stunned her into silence.

"If I die," Gloria confessed, "I'm afraid that people will lose their faith."

*   *   *

Her name was Bridgette until she was born. Then Dad cradled his little girl for the first time, and her beauty swayed him to make a revision.

"Gloria," Doug called her.

Mom cooed. The name was vintage, yet proper. She looked like a

Gloria. Not that they knew too many Glorias, but it felt almost ordained when Doug blurted the name.

"It was like God whispered in his ear," Kristen said.

Her first six years were storybook wonderful. Gloria was a character. On her second birthday, she climbed on the table, put a hand in her cake and commenced a messy, sugary feast. During Gloria's potty-training days, Diane Strauss, her paternal grandmother, warned her, "I'm gonna spank your bottom if you wet your bed tonight."

Replied Gloria: "You'll get your hand wet."

Grandma laughed. Gloria knew how to make heavy situations lighter.

Doug referred to her as his little flower child, and at first Kristen squirmed over the label because it carries a hippie connotation. But the husband offered a modified definition for Gloria: a curious little girl who enjoys the simplicity of life, who fantasizes about adventure, who loves the brilliance of colors, who gazes at a single flower and sees the whole garden.

Oh, what an imagination she possessed. She was so consumed with daydreams that her parents would have to call her multiple times to get her attention.

"There's our world, and then there's Gloria's world," Doug would often say. "She's right there with you, but she's not there with you."

When she began speaking, she had trouble saying words beginning with a "tr" sound. She pronounced them with an "f" sound. Her parents, still in their twenties, young and silly, couldn't resist asking her to say "truck."

Even when rearranging consonants, Gloria carried a sweet innocence. She never misbehaved in church. She revered priests. Whenever grownups talked about the concept of the Body of Christ, Gloria looked at them and then looked beyond them, trying to picture an actual body.

She would come to comprehend that phrase soon enough, however. Her childhood lasted but six years, really. By the time she turned seven, life began moving at a terrifying pace.

*   *   *

Her suffering began with a black eye. A soccer ball struck Gloria on the left side of her face, and strangely, the discoloration persisted for weeks. Why, her parents kept wondering. Why?

Sitting at the breakfast table one morning, Kristen gazed upon a most frightening sight: Gloria's eyes were drooping. Later, Gloria began experiencing leg pain that made it difficult to walk. It was time to see a doctor.

The first doctor theorized that Gloria's black eye was a sinus infection, and her legs ached from growing pains. He gave her some antibiotics. Ten days passed, and nothing had changed. He gave her more antibiotics. Ten more days passed, and nothing had changed. The parents called their friends for help finding another doctor.

In the middle of the uncertainty, Gloria celebrated her seventh birthday. Kristen bought flashlights for all the guests at the party, props for a game called Sardines they would play that night. Sardines was a twist on hide-and-seek: One person hid, and those who found the hidden person also squeezed into the hiding place. The game continued until only one person was left searching, and in the process, the hiding kids would resemble sardines bunched into a can.

It was the "funnest time ever" many of the young guests raved, after dashing through darkness for several hours. It also matched the daredevil within Gloria, as she always liked to push the boundaries of security. At a scary time—plagued by an invincible black eye and pondering possible diagnoses—it figured Gloria would use a spooky game to bide her time. Gloria, worry? Life thrilled her too much.

And then she learned she was seriously ill.

Two weeks after Gloria's birthday, the Strausses went to Virginia Mason Medical Center in their hometown of Federal Way, Washington, where the doctor greeted them with great concern.

"Can you go to Children's Hospital tomorrow?" he asked.

On the drive to Children's, which required a thirty-minute commute to Seattle, Gloria surprised her mother with a question.

"Why does God let kids get sick?"

Mom had no definitive answer, and instead of fibbing, she told Gloria as much. So the child roamed onto another subject, enjoying the quality time, oblivious to the ensuing peril.

After arriving at Seattle Children's Hospital, they walked past the cancer unit, and Kristen noticed all the bald-headed kids, feeling both sympathy and relief. *We've been so blessed that our kids don't have problems*, she told herself. She never questioned why they were there.

Looking back, Kristen figures this was God's way of keeping her calm, helping her handle the trauma to come. She had been through enough, for certain. Four months prior, she was bedridden, enduring an extreme exacerbation of a disease that hounded her—multiple sclerosis. To feel healthy again, to be active, was a blessing. Kristen was too busy cherishing the simple joys of normalcy to hunt for more despair. With roses blooming in her life, she didn't care to sniff around for garbage.

The Children's doctors looked at Gloria's face. Her black eye was mostly gone, but she still had a large bump over her left eyebrow. They did some tests and came to a somber conclusion.

Gloria has cancer, they said.

What kind, they didn't know. Maybe leukemia. Maybe something called Ewing's sarcoma or neuroblastoma. They told Gloria to return on Monday for an official diagnosis.

It was a Friday, so the limbo would last through the weekend. The Strauss family knew it had met an unforgettable day: March 7, 2003. The only question was whether that date signified a beginning or an end.

*　*　*

That weekend, the Strausses prepared themselves. Kristen called her mother and came away with a mantra.

"We have to put on our armor," Kristen kept repeating.

Kristen hoped it was not leukemia. She had heard about leukemia, and nobody wants leukemia. Ewing's sarcoma? She didn't want Gloria to have that, either, but it seemed more manageable than leukemia.

Neuroblastoma? It was a mystery to the family. But what could be worse than leukemia?

As the Strausses awaited the verdict, God pre-empted the silence. During prayer one night, Kristen heard a voice deliver a startling message.

Your daughter will have an incurable disease. When I heal her, I will change the lives of many.

The mother was horrified, yet comforted. What a revelation this was: a nightmare wrapped with fantasy, danger laced with the guarantee of safety. Kristen didn't know whether to be mournful or elated, not to mention stunned over experiencing a real-life God moment. She had always been sincere in her Catholic faith, but here was God, offering previews of Gloria's life.

A few days later, part of the premonition became a fact. Doctors took a biopsy of the growth on Gloria's face and put it under the microscope. Her wound had just been stitched when the results arrived. Gloria had an incurable cancer: neuroblastoma.

Kristen learned neuroblastoma would be far more sinister than leukemia. The diagnosis was harsh: an advanced stage four, thirty percent chance of living. The droopy eyes—that was cancer. The pain in her legs—that was cancer.

We will start chemotherapy tomorrow, the doctors said. The Strausses were ready. They came to the hospital with packed bags.

Neuroblastoma is as heinous as it sounds. It is a disease of the sympathetic nervous system, the village of nerves in the body that transmit messages from the brain. It tortures only children, slithering and hiding and gaining strength until conquering the vital organs, playing its own deadly game of Sardines. Discover it early, and the survival rate is high. However, some children fend off the symptoms for a while, which complicates their condition. If Gloria had been diagnosed before turning five, the odds would have favored her. At seven, her life was beginning to leak away.

"But I'm not going to lose my hair, right?" she asked her parents when they tried to explain her illness.

Doug and Kristen looked up at their daughter. Their facial expressions gave away the answer.

"Well, honey, you probably will," Kristen replied.

That was the first time neuroblastoma made Gloria cry.

Doug looked at his sullen, nervous family and decided to be bold. He knew he had to do something. His wife was stressed and about to wrestle with thoughts of Gloria's death. Doug and Kristen had four other children, too, none older than nine, and Kristen was pregnant with their sixth child. Three years later, they would welcome a seventh into the world. With a large family, Dad could envision disarray if he didn't set the agenda.

"I declare a breakthrough for our family," he said. "I'm not sure what that is, but our family will not be destroyed by this."

Over the next six months, leading into the stem-cell transplant, Gloria's life sped up, accelerating at an incomprehensible pace, hardship and happiness trying to outdo each other along the way. Her support group multiplied from dozens to hundreds. Her personality, bright as a halogen light, went from cute to inspirational.

When Gloria dreaded chemotherapy, her family referenced *Star Wars*, one of her obsessive joys at the time. Everyone told her to think of the chemo as the Jedi, and its mission was to defeat the Sith, or the cancer, and save her body. Gloria enjoyed the analogy, and it quelled her concern until her hair started falling out. Then she would spend hours using duct tape to pick every loose hair off her pillow.

But there were happier moments, so joyful that Gloria helped her family coin a nickname for the hospital. The Strausses called it "Hotel Children's Hospital" and sang it to the melody of the Eagles' song "Hotel California." They treated the nurses like family members and built an incredible kinship through the unfortunate circumstances. With Gloria as the star, the cast was always in harmony.

Gloria perfected all of Michael Jackson's dance moves as a way to exercise while recovering after chemotherapy. The nurses, her audience, would laugh at the performance. Doug made a video of it, and the recording revealed a touching scene: a girl, bony from her ordeal, standing on a hospital bed and grooving with a baseball hat covering her bald head, glowing despite pale skin.

During another of her dozens of hospital stays, she opened her eyes to a room full of gifts. Though she cherished the love of her family and friends, she felt unfairly doused with affection and gave some of her presents to neighboring patients. Those were the types of moments that helped Kristen come to an answer to her daughter's question.

Why does God let kids get sick? Well, Kristen figured, He chooses people strong enough to handle the pain, and then He takes their suffering and uses it for good. The good had come in droves. Gloria's anguish was the panacea for the unconcerned and unmoved, for those wandering through life without purpose. It seemed all who met Gloria wanted to pray for her and pray with her, regardless of the strength of their spiritual conviction. It seemed everyone wanted to do something to help, whether it was cooking a meal for the family, offering to pay a bill, or baby-sitting the other children. They felt like they needed to be close to this situation, felt like they were near something special, even if they did not quite understand it. Gloria had a transforming power within her, an ability to inspire with her grace, an influence so strong it made people unable to retreat to the frivolity in their lives. The image of a girl, straining to live, proclaiming what Mom told her—*God said a miracle is coming!*—was too powerful to ignore.

Somehow, the Strausses refrained from scrutinizing the tenuous language of their hope. *When I heal her, I will change the lives of many.* If God had spoken those words during a press conference, he would have needed to answer follow-up questions for two hours. When exactly would "when" be? How will you heal her? Why, of all the sick people in the world, will you heal Gloria? Whose lives will be changed? What comes first: the healing or the lives changing?

The Strausses were refreshingly different, at least when it came to God. It helped that Gloria was a first-grader. She enjoyed a filial faith. She could believe in her religion, her miracle, without hesitation. God would heal her because Mom said so, and that was that. Throughout her suffering, Gloria kept this amazing focus.

* * *

The stem-cell transplant came with two great risks. Gloria could die during the procedure. And there was fear her body would be put through Hell in vain, and she would endure a slow, tormenting downfall.

The latter turned out to be her predicament. The new stem cells couldn't get rid of her disease. As cancer raised tents inside her body, doctors were forced to make a dire prediction: She had anywhere from three months to three years to live.

Dr. Julie Park, Gloria's oncologist and a relentless combatant of neuroblastoma, detailed additional medical options, including experimental drugs. Doug and Kristen followed her suggestions. They trusted her, and furthermore, they anticipated Gloria's miracle. The first part of God's preview, the incurable disease, had come true. The healing and lives changing could not come soon enough.

Dr. Park concocted a suitable combination of experimental drugs, and Gloria's cancer went dormant for a few years. Freed from despair, she played soccer, basketball and volleyball. She stood in front of the mirror and played diva. She dazzled her friends with her rallying abilities, rising from patient to congenial student.

Maybe the miracle would materialize, after all.

When Kristen first received God's message, she was careful not to share it with too many people. She didn't want to make a bold declaration, didn't want to be judged. It took a conversation with her mother to garner enough courage to fully embrace the thought of a miracle.

Kristen called her mother, Vicki Trimberger, to share thoughts she'd been having of Gloria's death. Her anxiety threatened to block out the heavenly edict.

"Stop that," Vicki urged her daughter. "You claim what you heard."

After she claimed it, Kristen began receiving mystical pep talks. The most prominent came when she was in the kitchen, perplexed over the healing promise, thinking to herself, *Am I making this up?* She prayed for an answer. The response was a voice telling her to read a piece of scripture, Matthew 10.

"Matthew 11?" she wondered aloud.

Matthew 10, the voice reaffirmed. Kristen went to the bedroom to find her Bible. This was a treasured possession, a gift from her late grandmother, Mary Louise Miller, her spiritual role model. Grandma Miller died in 1998, and even though several years had passed, Kristen still found herself clinging to this Bible, remembering Grandma's example and imagining how she might attack Gloria's illness.

Kristen flipped through the pages in search of the scripture, and when she reached it, she was shocked to see three verses underlined in that chapter, Matthew 10:1, 7–8. Kristen read the material carefully and discovered it was a lesson about healing.

> 1 *Then he summoned his twelve disciples and gave them authority to expel unclean spirits and to cure sickness and disease of every kind.*
>
> 7 *As you go, make this announcement: 'The reign of God is at hand!'*
>
> 8 *Cure the sick, raise the dead, heal the leprous, expel the demons. The gift you have received, give as a gift.*

Kristen rested the open Bible in her lap and wept. Later, she wrote about the moment in her journal and wept some more. From that point on, she never hesitated to claim Gloria's miracle.

CHAPTER TWO

THE REPORTER

I won her story. Gloria was the spoils of a coin-flip triumph. Don Shelton, an assistant sports editor, knew the skeleton of a nice feature: A high school basketball coach named Doug Strauss was on a fifteen-game winning streak despite having a daughter with cancer and a wife with MS. Who wants it?

Heck, who doesn't want it? It was like someone had invented cavity-free candy. I expressed the most intrigue, along with my colleague, Steve Kelley. We were the sports columnists for *The Seattle Times*, and we both liked to mix opinions with human-interest tales. It was late January 2007, so football season was almost over, basketball was at midseason, and baseball had yet to begin. Something fresh was needed, and besides, I had just turned twenty-nine, which meant I was going through a my-life-should-have-more-meaning-because-I'm-almost-thirty phase. As a sports journalist, I guessed writing a piece without a score in it would be a promising start.

Because we were both so interested, Don threw a nickel into the air to decide who would get the story. Steve called tails. When Don took his top hand off the coin, we saw Thomas Jefferson's face.

Steve threw his hands up in playful disgust. I laughed. I won. I was ready to wax about the wondrous healing powers of sports, ready to use cancer and MS as props, ready to till the soil to plant another tale of overcoming obstacles. After all, these kinds of stories were the changeup du jour in sports journalism.

Tired of the triviality of athletics? Find a tragedy with a sports connection, and then use it to make the game seem as important as it needs to be. Consider it jumper cables for the guilty sports enthusiast.

I was so excited that I didn't call Doug Strauss for three weeks. Guess I really wasn't excited. Blame laziness. Blame an inability to break from routine. Blame trepidation over having to write about the sick. It had to be some combination of those three, or maybe some part of me sensed this would be more than the customary tearjerker.

*   *   *

At last, I called Doug Strauss. He was the boys basketball coach at John F. Kennedy High School in nearby Burien. He also taught math and Spanish at Kennedy, the place where he fell in love with Kristen. We agreed to meet during his planning period on February 21.

Doug was different. He just happened to be a coach. He stood 5-foot-9, giggled often and spoke faster than a cheetah on a lunch run. As we wandered the halls of the high school, students exclaimed "Strauss! Strauss!" as they passed him. Doug joked with two lovebirds about giving up kissing for Lent. He was part teacher, part coach and part comedian.

The kids loved Doug, just not as much as they loved Gloria. Most every locker was decorated with a flier featuring the girl's picture and the words "Glorified by Gloria." The students also made pink paper chains full of well-wishes. Doug grinned as he admired their signs of compassion.

"I came in today and just saw this," he said, touching a chain. "I didn't know they were going to do this."

"It's pretty amazing that all these teenagers love your little girl so much," I replied.

"Kennedy is, like, an extension of our family," Doug said. "Kristen and I are both alums. We met here. We started dating the second half of our senior year, back in '92, and we never looked back. The first time we went out, I went home and said, 'Mom, this is someone I want to marry.' It was just meant to be."

Doug interrupted himself. "Yesterday was Gloria's birthday. Did you know that? She's eleven now. We pray that she sees many more years."

We chatted for about thirty more minutes, mostly about the school. Kristen's father, Pat Trimberger, graduated from Kennedy, too. Doug was baptized here during his junior year, at the gymnasium, before the entire school, and he still counted the moment as the most profound event of his life. Kennedy felt more like a Strauss family estate than a high school.

When Doug finished reminiscing, the day's final bell rang, and it was time for basketball practice. I asked if I could watch and finish the interview later.

During slow moments in the workout, I looked behind me at the JFK alma mater posted on the wall. Most school songs are too cheesy to digest, and maybe this one was, too. Still, I was inspired. The lyrics seemed a little more authentic, a little more worthwhile. I had to scribble down the words.

> As day fades into evening,
> Fond memories we will share,
> Of moments that we cherish,
> Our friendships while we are there,
> The lessons we have learned from you,
> Will always be inside,
> You'll always be a part of us,
> You'll always be our guide,

No matter where life takes us,
Our home will always be,
Our friend and alma mater,
John F. Kennedy.

After practice, the father opened up about Gloria's current problem. A few weeks ago, Dr. Park told Gloria her cancer was spiking. The dormant period was long over, and Dr. Park needed to try something different to slow the disease. Her solution, for now, was to give the child an antibody with a chemo agent. Beginning the next week, Gloria would be forced to make the hospital a second home again. She was most upset over all the school time she would have to miss.

Gloria had outlived the prediction of three months to three years that came after her stem-cell transplant failed to work. The cancer around her eye was mostly gone. Her legs felt fine. She was living normally. Now her sneaky disease had her cornered again.

"She's already kind of a miracle," Doug said of his daughter. "So now we're at the point where it's, 'Here we go again.' She was down and out four years ago. Our family has had a lot of adversity, but we've really managed to stick together. Through God and through our friends' support, we've made a breakthrough out of all our issues. Thank God for all of that. Who knows where we'd be without God?"

*   *   *

When Doug said that name—God—it moved me. I hadn't been affected like that for years, not by someone spiritual. In my world, I often listened to professional athletes thank God for everything from their new contracts to their new mistresses. I had become desensitized to their gospel. I had become desensitized to God in general.

I knew better than to scrimp the Lord. I was taught better. I am the grandson of a Baptist minister, and on both sides of my family, there was an expectation to attend church regularly, to praise God for all things— including my beating heart and new shoes and passing algebra tests without studying—and to read and comprehend the Bible.

During high school, my pastor gave me the pulpit twice to speak during special church celebrations. For Men's Day, I talked about changing from a boy to a man. For Youth Day, I discussed lessons learned from Cain and Abel and punctuated my remarks about the ills of jealousy by repeatedly saying, "Yes, you Cain," as if to tell onlookers to stop thinking like Cain. As an eighteen-year-old, I thought it was so clever. Barack Obama had nothing on me.

Then I went to college. And fell in love. And fell out of love. And strayed from God because of it.

She believed the Bible dictated we couldn't be together. I'm black, she's white, and somewhere in the Good Book, the Lord apparently said interracial dating was as perilous as text-messaging while driving.

"Where does it say that?" I asked angrily.

"I can't tell you exactly," she said. "My dad quoted it to me last night."

I had never been more furious. I had never been more heartbroken, either. It hurt so much I didn't bother casting the disappointment as the ignorance of a rogue worshipper wanting to cram prejudice into the Bible. I'd met this man, liked him, thought he liked me. So rather than challenge his misguided logic, I allowed it to hover over me, turning my spirit dark, making me question Christianity.

Pretty soon, the doubts grew so strong it was hard to be around church folks. They were all starting to resemble the maniacs who stand in public with signs and megaphones, screaming at pedestrians, telling them they will go to Hell if they don't bow before God right this minute.

So church kept falling down my list, sinking from a lesser priority to a nuisance to nothing. There was too much studying, too much partying, too much rebellion. I was too intelligent for my own spirit. Sometimes, religion didn't make logical sense, and that was when trust needed to kick in, but I didn't have that trust anymore. Besides, what scholar could abandon intellect? It was so much easier to drink another beer.

I got by just fine for several years. Graduated from college. Took jobs in Philadelphia, Orlando, Louisville and Seattle. Promoted to the coveted position of columnist at age twenty-five. My career progressed at an astounding pace, but the only problem was that I awoke every morning feeling a crippling level of dissatisfaction. The funk was inescapable, and professional success couldn't stymie it. In fact, achievements fueled the discontent.

Six months after moving to Seattle, just days before meeting Doug, I sat in my car as tears rolled down my face like marbles on linoleum floors, so unrestrained they forced me to stop driving. I pulled into the parking lot of a Walgreens store and wept and wept and wept as the U2 song "One" wailed through the speakers. When it finished playing, I pecked at the CD player to repeat the number. I am not sure how many times I did that. I can only tell you "One" lasted long enough for me to drench both ends of my sleeves from wiping my eyes.

Something about the lyrics haunted and inspired me. When the song felt melancholy, it changed and surged with hope. When it felt hopeful, it changed and lumbered through despair. Ultimately, it was an encouraging song about unity, I guessed, but the feeling within the words, the way Bono longed for them, seized the essence of my conflict. I wanted to be whole. Unlike U2, however, I had no conduit for my message, just a loneliness I couldn't release.

"What do you want from me?" I cried out, on the verge of hyperventilating. "What did I do wrong, God? What the Hell is going on?"

It was the disappointment of another love lost mixed with the isolation I felt being in Seattle, 2,300 miles from my Kentucky home. It was the realization that ambition failed to fulfill me, for it only left me telling the stories of strangers and stonewalling myself, the curse of an imbalanced journalist. It was nothing new—familiar worries, a depression I had stifled for years. This time, however, the emotions refused to be stashed away.

"I'm trying, but it won't stop," I said, sniffling. "I just want it to stop."

I wondered if the world would miss me if I skipped the rest of my life. If I were so bold, I had the perfect plan: run my stupid, oversized white Cadillac Escalade over the 520 bridge and into Lake Washington. Only

I was not that bold and therefore doomed to be the saddest man ever to own a Caddy.

"I need something," I begged.

I was speaking to God, I think. It had been a while.

"Something!"

* * *

I loved listening to Doug talk. Really, there was no choice but to listen. He had a runaway brain; his mind skipped from subject to subject without any logical transitions. He was a mouth without brakes.

He was fascinating, though, because his chatter came with tender perspective, humility and brave aspiration. This story involved much more than sports, and after his team made a surprising early exit from the playoffs, I had a clear path to think bigger. It was just what I needed. It was something truly fresh, not another trite tale to justify covering athletics.

Doug and I met five times over the next two months before I was even introduced to Gloria. We would fall into deep conversations over coffee or lunch or tea. We would stay for three or four hours, covering topics such as fatherhood, poverty, the real meaning of joy and, of course, religion.

Doug talked unlike any man I had met. It was like his vocal chords were extra arteries, transmitting every message within his heart. He kept mentioning how he had to give up his righteousness to help his family.

"That's hard for a man to do," he said. "We like to think we have all the answers. We like to think we can do everything to protect and provide for our family. You can't always be right. Sometimes, you have to say you're sorry, or you need help. And being emotional is OK. I love to hug, love to kiss. I admit that my wife is the pillar when it comes to our family's faith. This is no time for righteousness and ego."

Seconds later, Doug was singing.

"Heaven musta sent you from abuhhhhhhvvvvvve! You know that song? It's Marvin Gaye, right? I tell Kristen that song's for her. I won the wife lottery. If you ever get married, be sure to use that line. I won the wife lottery. Now, I mean it every time I say it, but in case you're wondering, 'What's something nice I can say to my wife?' Remember: I won the wife lottery."

I laughed and moved onto the next question, but Doug interrupted.

"Seven kids, I must've said 'I won the wife lottery' a lot."

Doug also boasted about how he once ended an argument with Kristen by trimming a bush into the shape of a heart.

We were fast becoming friends because nothing about Doug's life was off-limits. He admitted the family struggled to pay the bills. Before their family grew so large, Doug and Kristen agreed she would stay at home so the kids would have a strong relationship with their mother. Now, with a basketball team full of little Strausses, Kristen couldn't change her mind because the cost of childcare would be too outrageous. So nine people lived off a teacher's salary.

They refused to make money an issue, however. "If money's our problem, we don't have any problems," Doug said.

He joked that, when the phone company called demanding payment, he would reply, "Come on, man, my wife's got MS!" The representative would apologize and hang up.

To make extra money, Doug worked at the famous Pike Place Market in Seattle as one of the fish guys, tossing, cleaning and preparing fish. He loved the job, and he returned every year as much for the camaraderie as the paycheck. The fish guys were a special group, a tight group. They talked about being better men. A man named John Christensen even produced a film and series of books to document their philosophies. Doug enjoyed saying his perspective was steeped in Catholicism and fish.

"I want this to be a positive experience," Doug said as he recited his research about high divorce rates when parents care for terminally ill children. "Sometimes, you want to feel sad. Sometimes, you want to have a pity party. I don't like saying I worry about her dying, but I do. It's only human. We can't lose sight of that miracle, though."

He paused, stared out the window and grinned. He remembered a quote from Mother Teresa: When we suffer, it's God kissing us. Then he let out a good chuckle.

"Sometimes, we wish God would stop kissing us."

* * *

Our most emotional conversation came on April 19. We were at a Starbucks, and we both needed to leave in an hour. Instead, we talked for nearly three. Doug trusted me. He kept introducing his feelings with the phrase, "Since I trust you," which could be interpreted as an endorsement and a warning to do right by him. He also kept talking about this eerie television moment he experienced.

Doug had seen it a few weeks ago, but he could not shake the memory. He was watching the tube alone late one March night. A little girl, about eight, appeared on this infomercial for St. Jude's Hospital. She looked just like Gloria. Doug was hooked.

He learned her story. The girl had cancer, and at the end of the show, she died. Then the narrator said, "Neuroblastoma still eludes us."

"No!" Doug exclaimed.

He thought to himself, *If my daughter dies, am I going to have faith?*

He slept little that night and went to school in the morning. Because it was Lent, Doug read spiritual lessons from a pamphlet to his class each day. That day's lesson concluded with a summary that rocked him as much as that infomercial.

It read: "You have to turn to God, during good or bad, even when you lose a child to cancer."

He stood before his class and cried, long and hard.

Now he was reliving the experience with me because he felt a defining moment was nearing. He sensed she was hiding something.

"Something we don't know," he said. "She's holding onto stuff—that's my fear."

As we talked for those three hours, we realized that we understood each other. We knew that, over the course of two months, this story had transcended sports, transcended illness, transcended the ambiguity of faith, and we were taking a one-way trip to God. The newspaper story had to revolve around waiting for Him to heal Gloria.

"It's nice to be able to share my faith," Doug said. "Sometimes, you get in the public world, and you don't say 'God.' You're scared to say 'God.' But it's a huge part of our success as a family, and God has to be included in this story."

I nodded. How I could make this work, how I could write a narrative starring The Big Character in the Sky, I didn't know. However, ignoring Him would be a false depiction. His presence was too strong in the Strausses' lives, and He was the only way to do this story justice.

I saw a bit of myself in Doug. We were close in age; he was four years older. We were unapologetically sensitive men. We were attracted to strong women. Our biological fathers had abandoned us, but our mothers married men who filled the void so well that we called them Dad and never longed for our blood papas. The only difference was that, while Doug's faith was like an express train, mine was a jalopy parked in the backyard. I knew it was there and pondered fixing it, but riding in something else was too easy.

Doug mentioned these dynamic prayer sessions his community hosted. He said he would invite me to the next one. Sure, I told him with faux enthusiasm, I will be there.

He caught on to the phony excitement and said laughingly, "All right, I'm going to hold you to that."

*   *   *

The next day, on a Friday morning drive to school, Doug listened to a voicemail from Dr. Park, heard the urgency and worry in her voice, and prepared himself. He knew to expect the worst. She was away in Texas, and Doug knew she wouldn't call about something insignificant. He sighed and dialed the numbers. He got her voicemail. He turned his car around and went home.

Doug was overwhelmed. How would he handle the news? How could he make this breakdown a breakthrough? He turned up the radio as he drove. He was tuned to 1050 AM, and his friend, Tom Curran, who runs a Catholic ministry, was in the middle of his show. The first words Doug heard Tom say to his audience: "Hand it all over to God."

A few hours later, Dr. Park called back. Gloria's cancer was everywhere. It was in her liver, lymph nodes, bones and bone marrow. Dr. Park estimated the child had weeks to live, possibly as short as a month. This was the moment the family always feared. From the beginning, the Strausses had a feeling the miracle would come at a critical time and braced for major torment while they waited, but they weren't ready for the endgame.

Gloria was good at defying medical timelines. Still, the new window was frighteningly imminent. And Doug was home alone. The kids were at school, Kristen was out running errands, and they all were scheduled to arrive at the same time. Doug had to figure out how to tell his wife without scaring the kids. Fortunately, Gloria wasn't with the family; she was to spend the night at a friend's house.

He called Kristen's cell phone a few minutes before she was due home. "I have a surprise for you," he said. "Just drop the kids off. Don't even get out of the car."

After the kids greeted their father and raced into the house, Doug told them, "Hey, I need to take Mommy. There's something special I want to show her."

Doug asked his wife to drive a few blocks away to his favorite meditation spot, a place where the Puget Sound seemingly flows right into your eyes. He broke down and cried as he relayed what Dr. Park said. She cried, too, but then her mood turned as calm as the Sound.

"The time is now," she said. "It's what we've been preparing for. It's now really God. It's just Him. There's a miracle that can be performed."

A day earlier, Kristen and Gloria had a deep discussion about her illness. For two months, Gloria had been on a dizzying medical merry-go-round, in and out of the hospital, hoping something would slow the cancer.

They knew the latest round of tests would provide definitive answers, so Kristen approached her daughter with a scenario.

"Let's play What If. What if it's bad news?"

Gloria responded quickly. "Well, I'll have a good cry, but I kind of feel like it's going to get worse before it gets better."

That same day, Gloria planned the sleepover at Aleah Ruth's house. Aleah was one of Gloria's best friends, a fellow fifth-grader at St. Philomena Catholic School, and her mother, Mary Ruth, taught sixth grade at St. Phil. The girls met in kindergarten, and by the third grade, their bond had grown deeper than most elementary-school friendships. Aleah admired Gloria's talent for remaining cordial despite her medical problems, for being a peacemaker during fights and for wanting to be a prayer leader in class.

Because Aleah's birthday party was that Saturday, Gloria wanted to spend extra time with her friend the night before. On Friday evening, as the girls played with their dolls and Build-a-Bears, Mary received a call from Doug while she cooked. He asked if the girls were nearby. She said no. He requested that she make sure Gloria could not overhear the call, and after Mary's assurances, Doug told her of "the worst news any parent could hear." Mary leaned against a wall and slid down slowly, like a trickle of water. The next thing she knew, she was on the floor. Doug was still debating whether to come get Gloria, but he instructed Mary to act normal. She was devastated, but she agreed.

After they hung up, Mary and her husband looked out the window, at two girls pushing a doll stroller up the block, one healthy, one fading. Mary couldn't imagine Aleah without Gloria, couldn't imagine the Ruth household without Gloria.

Doug and Kristen decided to keep their daughter happy for one more night. Gloria enjoyed dinner with the Ruths, and later the girls set up sleeping bags on the floor of a playroom. They watched movies and ate snacks until they fell asleep at 10 p.m.

The next morning, Mary made them pancakes and asked Gloria

how she slept. Gloria admitted a stomachache bothered her all night. She had been having pain all month, but she barely mentioned it. A few days before, during a banquet for Doug's basketball team, she had joked with her grandmother, Diane Strauss, that the players looked silly walking with fake limps, trying to be cool.

"Their legs aren't even hurting like mine, and they walk like their legs hurt," she said.

Beyond that, Gloria suffered in silence.

After Gloria mentioned she was awake throughout the night, Mary asked why she didn't wake up someone in the house. Gloria said she didn't want to bug anyone.

After finishing breakfast, they headed to Laser Quest for Aleah's birthday. As children and parents gathered for high-tech games of hide-and-seek, Mary struggled to conceal the news. She saw Lori Rosellini, one of Kristen's closest friends, and her daughter, Lexie. The mothers shared a knowing look.

When the kids went into the Laser Quest room, Mary broke down and told two people. The three of them sobbed and quickly rubbed away their tears before the children returned. Gloria was having fun, but she looked exhausted. Mary noticed dark circles under her eyes. She was thirsty and kept asking for extra juice boxes. It became difficult for Mary not to analyze all of Gloria's actions and constantly ponder if she was OK, if she was comfortable.

The girls asked Mary to take some pictures. They all struck a "Charlie's Angels" pose. Precious, Mary thought. These could be the last normal hours of Gloria's life.

When Kristen came to pick up Gloria, Mary hugged the distressed mother. "How will you tell her?" she asked.

"We're still working on that," Kristen answered.

*   *   *

The parents called a family meeting. Gloria knew them too well; as soon as she saw the sad look on their faces, she spoke for them.

"I know," she said, crying.

With wet eyes looking back at her, Gloria unveiled her inner turmoil. She admitted to feeling badly for several weeks. She admitted to hiding pain in her legs and aches in her stomach. She admitted she wanted to skirt reality for as long as she could.

Doug hugged his daughter. "From now on, you've gotta promise to tell me when you're hurting."

Gloria kissed her father. "Promise."

For the next three days, the Strausses let their emotions flow unrestrained. Gloria couldn't remember seeing Dad cry much, so the sight of him sobbing uncontrollably would spark her tears. Doug and Kristen kept the kids out of school the first part of the next week, a decision they would be forced to make several more times. They needed to be together, and they needed to determine the next move.

Dr. Park still had options. She could continue searching for a winning combination with experimental drugs, but because the next trial might involve a strong dose of chemo, quality of life became an issue.

"I'm afraid to do something because I don't want to beat my body up with the medicine and not beat the cancer," Gloria said. "And I'm afraid to do nothing and just let the cancer grow."

From a medical standpoint, it seemed like the ultimate dilemma. So the Strausses leaned on their faith more than ever.

When I heal her, I will change the lives of many.

They opened their home to prayer every night, and friends flocked to join them. They asked God for a healing, but first they sought His input on whether to continue cancer treatment. They asked for the patience to get through this ordeal, for the family to remain bonded and for the intelligence to make the proper decisions.

Between tears, the calm Kristen experienced would flow through the rest of the family. Friends began feeling it, too. If they resisted the sadness, they received the reward. If they believed in the miracle, they noticed beauty amid the crisis.

The atmosphere at these prayer sessions became so enthralling that Doug wanted to capture it on videotape. So he asked Marc Sheehan, an old Kennedy High classmate, to record the proceedings one night. Marc agreed, though he barely knew how to operate Doug's camera. Instead of troubling his friend for instructions, Marc tried to figure it out himself.

He looked nervously through the lens and focused on Gloria, who was resting on the couch. While he played cameraman, he made a startling observation. He saw beams of light coming from the nearby Virgin Mary statuette and falling onto Gloria. At first, he considered it a trick of the light, but he thought it odd that other lit candles weren't creating the same effect in different parts of the room.

Later that evening, as he said goodbye, he told Doug and Kristen he wasn't sure what he had seen, but they should look at the tape. The video confirmed what Marc saw. Indeed, the beams looked as if they were flowing from the Virgin Mary to Gloria.

"Heaven touched Gloria," Marc would say every time he recounted the memory.

Doug cherished his home videos, and for him, this recording trumped all the others. He had documented Gloria's entire cancer battle, from the Michael Jackson performances to the birthday parties that were no longer promised. Gloria was embarrassed by some of those videos because they showed her sick or frail or bald, sometimes all three, but she appreciated the significance of what they captured.

When visitors stopped by, Dad wanted to throw in a tape and share the memories. Gloria pleaded for him to show the times when she looked good. She had yet to comprehend that, though she was movie-star pretty, her acts were more striking.

Mostly, the father watched these videos while alone, late at night, and then he raved to everyone else about what Gloria did on tape. After he saw those beams of light, he called me, talking faster than ever, saying he knew God was close during those prayer sessions, relishing the proof that had been uncovered.

"I wouldn't miss any more of this if I were you," he said.

Next time, I told him.

"Next time is tomorrow night!"

OK, the next, next time.

"You're welcome to come whenever. These prayer meetings for my little Geezy Deezy are incredible, I'm telling you."

I agreed to attend a prayer session that week, refused to commit to when, but told Doug he could count on my attendance.

"You'd better watch out!" Doug exclaimed. "There might have to be prayer in *The Seattle Times*. Your paper will never be the same."

I countered by telling Doug that my newspaper was open to depicting all compelling aspects of life. The company line was delivered without a stutter.

"I've never seen it before," Doug responded. "Not like what we're doing."

"Well, that's why I'm doing this," I told him.

Behind those words, however, I was unsure whether the story would be embraced inside my newsroom. I was unsure whether I had embraced it just yet, but it felt too spectacular, too moving to ignore. I had to make the leap. During my two months of taking stealthy footsteps around the Strausses, the intrigue had tripled. If I waited any longer, Gloria might die before I finished the story.

It was time to meet her. It was time to stop being scared and to completely immerse myself.

* * *

Tragedy lurked, but the Strausses still thought differently. They still thought "miracle." But they were not foolish and knew to prepare for anything. For Doug and Kristen, it was a vexing conundrum: Their brains were split between miracle and mayhem, but their hearts belonged to God's promise.

When I heal her, I will change the lives of many.

Two of the Strauss boys, three-year-old Sam and five-year-old Anthony, walked into the den one day while Doug was crying.

"Did Mom die?" Sam asked.

No, Dad told him, he was crying about Gloria's cancer. Sam gave his father a hug. Anthony came over to comfort him, too.

"I know what you want, Dad," Anthony said. "You want to get Gloria a present."

As Doug listened to his son, Anthony grew more confident.

"I know what you want," Anthony continued. "I know what you want! You want to go see *Teenage Mutant Ninja Turtles* and then go get her a present!"

Doug grabbed Anthony, held him and laughed.

Gloria strikes one of her many poses. She often wondered if modeling could be a possible avenue to stardom. © Paul Dudley

CHAPTER THREE

RED CARPET

Gloria walked into my life hiding a limp. She took slow, rhythmic, graceful steps. As she moved from a white van toward the house, it seemed merely as if she were lost in her imagination, not ill but in an elegant daydream, a glamour girl parading into a classy affair.

I was fooled, for certain. This was not the image of a dying child. If she was ill, then I never had met healthy. Gloria radiated poise in this chaotic moment. The entire Strauss family—two parents, seven children, nine lives—had emerged from the van and scurried inside, an hour and a half tardy for our meeting. Some were sprinting. Some were speed-walking. Some were colliding. Gloria sauntered inside, in gorgeous defiance of her plight.

She was as precious as her father described. When she smiled, joy overtook her face. Her cheeks creased into a half moon, and they rose so high it made her big, blue eyes squint. Her teeth, a hodgepodge of baby and permanent, magnified her unfettered innocence. Then there was her skin, a pinch darker than the prototypical fair blonde, slightly bronzed, attracting every nearby ray.

It took a single glimpse to understand her nickname—Glow. The husband of Kristen's good friend, Lori Rosellini, gave her that moniker. Adam Rosellini looked at the child one day and said, "Hey, Glow!"

"My name's Gloria," she replied.

"I know but you glow like an angel," Adam countered. "Can I call you Glow?"

Gloria was unsure. "I'm Geezy Deezy," she told him. "That's what my dad calls me. But if you want to, you can, I guess."

After some time, Gloria became fond of Glow. It was perfect. Light hit her differently. It did not just strike her in a flattering manner; she absorbed it. It was as if she possessed an internal spotlight.

"Helllloooo," she said softly, loitering in the greeting.

"H-Hi," I replied, extending my hand.

My nerves danced the foxtrot. All week, I had dreaded this encounter. I find it hard enough to talk to children, let alone an eleven-year-old with a terminal illness. How do you have an engaging conversation when mortality has its chin on your shoulder? None of my journalism experiences had prepared me for this task. This was not sports. This really mattered. I spoke with caution.

"It's really nice to meet you, Gloria. Your dad has told me so much about you."

She grinned and headed for her bedroom. That was when the limp became noticeable. No longer self-conscious, Gloria succumbed to the pain in her left leg as she left the room. Still, the irregular gait only made her look injured. Sprained ankle, maybe. Pulled hamstring, tops. How could this sweet child have cancer?

The house was too abuzz to ponder the question. Hard to believe now that, for an hour and a half, this place sat in near silence. When I arrived, two women were cleaning. Family friends, they told me, just trying to make life easier. The Strausses were still at Mass, would be home any minute, they said. Have a seat. They retreated to their chores and left me to my curiosity.

The decorations told the Strausses' story. A banner reading "God Bless Gloria" took up nearly two of their walls, with get-well notes filling the white space on the sign. A piano rested on the opposite wall, with a Virgin Mary statuette next to a stunning framed picture of Gloria. On the back of the front door, there was a white picture scroll commemorating the first Holy Communion of Maria Louise Strauss, the parents' nine-year-old daughter, the youngest girl. On the fireplace mantle, I looked at more images and guessed at matching the other kids' names. Alissa? Yes, the oldest, thirteen years old. Joe, the biggest boy, six years old. Anthony, a little smaller, five. Sam, even smaller, three. Vincent? The baby, seven months.

It took twenty minutes to be certain about all seven children. By the end of that exercise, my partner was pulling into the driveway. Steve Ringman had been tabbed as the photographer for this project. I had worked at the newspaper for eight months and never met him. He was a slender man with charcoal and silver hair, a simple dresser like most photographers, white button-down shirt, blue jeans, round glasses.

As we waited, we swapped stories. I shared my Kentucky roots; he spoke of growing up in Mount Vernon, Washington. I detailed my short career; he talked of photographing the Contra War in Nicaragua and earthquakes in El Salvador and San Francisco. He had just returned from Tanzania and Zambia, where he documented the malaria-relief efforts of the Bill and Melinda Gates Foundation.

We intersected at one thought: the state of our poor, sagging profession. Consider it financial cannibalism. The business model had collapsed. Ad revenue had decreased. The Internet had failed to make significant money. Antiquated, resistant to innovation, newspapers didn't even see the disaster coming. Now, they must tear their products apart just to survive. Now, they must make enemies of loyal journalists by cutting staff, shifting responsibilities and turning comprehensive daily news publications into something only good enough to provide them with a tomorrow.

"It sucks, doesn't it?" I asked Ringman.

"It's pretty grim, Jerry," he replied.

Working for a newspaper isn't a job. It's a compulsion, an unending quest to uncover every aspect of life, an addiction to dispatch new information again and again and again. You must be a few letters short of a full keyboard to want this lifestyle. The best of us lose ourselves in a probing, scrutinizing mindset, striving to be omniscient. We love our jobs, despite often grumbling otherwise, despite the unhealthy imbalance this work creates. We always want more, which is what makes our current state so depressing. It's no longer about the ideal of serving the truth and changing the world with each story. Cold, sterile business reigns. Those grumbles have become howls.

Into the middle of our professional depression stepped Gloria and her family. Our lament ended as soon as they arrived. The Strausses came home at the ideal time. The commotion was a virtue. With baby Vincent crying, with the three other boys running around, with the girls trying to police their brothers, newspaper angst withdrew from the scene.

The noise subsided as most of the kids wandered outside, but Gloria returned to the living room and sat beside her parents. It was April 26, Kristen's thirty-third birthday. She could've passed for 27, with her willowy frame that showed few signs of giving birth seven times, long hair the color of hay and eyes that smiled. Ringman and I marveled at her pleasant disposition. She was sugar with a heartbeat, sprinkling sweetness atop everyone she met.

Gloria bought her mother boots—brown ones with heels and straps—for her birthday. She saved money for months in order to afford them. Whenever someone gave her cash, she made certain to keep a chunk for Mom's gift. In fact, Gloria always plotted how she could afford to buy her family members something special.

Sitting in the Strauss house, I realized how silly it was for me to take so long to meet the whole family. They were wonderful people, somehow unburdened by their burden, warm and loving and goofy. I had expected a tense time. Perhaps I was worried, too, about handling the overarching themes of this tale: religion, cancer, death. On the drive from Seattle to the family's home, I repeated those words. Religion, cancer, death. Religion, cancer, death. Religion, cancer, death. Then I put them up against my normal subject matter.

Basketball, football, baseball. Religion, cancer, death.

For a few seconds, turning the car around became an option.

And then I met Gloria.

She settled in between her parents, legs dangling as she sat deep in the couch, and took over our conversation. She was the interviewer. We were all in her world.

"Do you, like, write about and take pictures of stars?" she asked.

Sometimes, but not really, we explained. We are not the paparazzi.

"I've always wanted to be a star."

She had the route planned. First, she would be on *American Idol*. That would prompt a singing career. Then she would venture into acting. That would make her versatile. And if she had time, maybe she could do some modeling. That would make her unforgettable.

"I have some songs picked out already," she said.

She took a breath and started to perform.

"I feel like a woman! I feel like a woman!" she cooed. "That's Shania Twain, I think. You know that song? One of them would definitely have to be, 'I Feel Like a Woman!'"

She hummed the melody some more and transitioned to the next song.

"Another one goes, 'Let's give them something to talk about,'" she sang, trying hard to sound like Bonnie Raitt.

I grinned and leaned forward. Ringman pointed his camera at Gloria but decided to enjoy the moment.

"Oh, and 'Livin' La Vida Loca' would be another one," Gloria said, mumbling the tune.

She was singing. She could not stop singing. She received a death sentence last week, and she was singing. Cancer had stalked her for almost four years, and she was singing. Pain made her left leg as stiff as lumber, and she was singing.

"I've always wanted to be a star."

Normally, she dreamed in the bathroom mirror. She saw her future with lavish clarity, visions so captivating they shrouded and muted all else. She treated that mirror as if it were a photographer's lens, turning and posing, kissing and waving.

She combed her closet to create unexpected combinations, to transform humble clothing pinched from the family's single income into fabulous finery. She arranged her hair to suit each fantasy—updo, elegant ponytail, straight and classic, wavy and wild. She would stand before the mirror for hours at a time. When her sisters asked what she was doing, she answered, "This is what the people in Hollywood are wearing."

Gloria was at the Academy Awards. She was at the Grammys. She was on *American Idol*.

When she bored of the celebrity routine, she played fashion designer and called on her sisters to model her attire. When Alissa and Maria wanted to escape from the fashionista, Gloria envisioned her prom night or dressed like a cowgirl, placing a toothpick in her mouth and using a fake country accent to reintroduce herself to the family. Oh, the impressions. She could mimic anyone after a few minutes of practice.

She was not the first child with a vibrant imagination. She was, however, blessed with a special flair that made her fantasies original.

"How do you become an actress at my age?" she asked her mother.

Before Kristen offered an answer, Gloria gave some pre-emptive persuasion.

"My dad says I'm not half bad at it."

We all laughed, nestled in Gloria's aspiration, safe from the dire circumstances that led to this gathering. However, Gloria knew to dream practically.

"I don't know if it'll happen down my line," she said, "but I hope it does."

CHAPTER FOUR

NO SPECTATORS

The Strausses lived in a white rambler tucked into a corner of Federal Way. The residence resembled a soldier in the push-up position, so long and narrow and flat. It sat hidden from drivers navigating twisty Dash Point Road, sequestered from plain view by trees. Even frequent visitors had trouble finding its entrance. There was just a sliver of a path.

This was my second trek to the Strauss house, yet I was lost again. The April dusk made it impossible to follow the last bit of Doug's directions: Keep winding until you see a posh, gated house on your left, turn there, make an immediate right and disappear, up a gravel ramp that curves into a driveway where kids dart about, playing games they invented five minutes ago.

It would've been wise to pay better attention while searching for that turn.

After missing the posh, gated house on the left by about three miles, I turned around, only to miss the posh, gated house again because you cannot see it traveling from the other direction. With one more U-turn, I solved the mystery, and then the jitters came.

It was my car. I was embarrassed to drive it. I felt like a pretentious punk bringing it here. In the narrow, tree-lined entrance to the Strauss house, my white Cadillac Escalade was a big, expensive, useless tank. If it came with facial expressions, it would have winced as limbs smacked against its windows, dirt ran up its sides and gravel crackled underneath its tires. The thought of being seen in this blasted thing made me more nervous than what I was visiting for: to attend a prayer session, at last. Here I was, squeezing this whale into the driveway of a family laboring to pay the bills and living in the most spiritual manner I had ever witnessed. It had to be the most humbling moment in the history of oversized, luxury sports-utility vehicles.

I parked and raced inside, same as I had done the first visit. People tend to talk about your car only when you are coming or going, and you hear none of it as long as you avoid loitering near your ride. I was happy to let this be the big, white Escalade in the driveway.

Besides, tonight was about prayer. I was here an hour early, enough time to chat with Alissa about cell phones (she wanted one badly) and independence and boys. She seemed uncomfortable during my first visit, so it was important to build a rapport. As we talked, I began to see Alissa as a thirteen-year-old version of Kristen. She was eerily identical to her mother, from her chatty, open-book style of conversation to her charming desire to do right in all situations. She just talked a lot faster than Mom, evidence of Doug's genes.

Alissa struggled to balance her craving for teenage freedom with wanting to spend as much time as possible with Gloria. She mentioned her boyfriend, but not with teen angst, instead presenting it as a simple, blossoming relationship. She loved school, detailed every subject with enthusiasm, and later, she sat at the piano to practice.

By the time we finished talking, visitors were arriving. Within thirty minutes, the living room was full, plump like a buffet belly. Forty people fit where they could, fit where they could not, in kitchen chairs, in desk chairs, on the piano bench, on the floor, on the fireplace hearth, against the wall, behind the couch, atop the coffee table. They gripped their rosaries and grinned upon eye contact. Prayer warriors, they called themselves. They were here for Gloria.

They wanted a miracle, or rather, they expected one. God will answer them. Gloria will live. Cancer will lose. Of these things, they were as certain as a grandparent's love. So they sat earnestly, waiting for Gloria to enter the room, preparing to unleash their hearts for yet another night.

What a mix of ambitious people: close friends, high school students, relatives, middle school students, church members, elementary school students, coaches, teachers, strangers. Over the next five months, prayer would saturate their lives, and the warriors would multiply, grow to incalculable numbers, forming a community that strode through each day with closed eyes and bowed heads, all because they believed this was the best way to cure Gloria.

Though the visitors changed, the living room had been jammed all week, and there was always a delayed start as Gloria stood in the bathroom, primping. She was cute enough to bypass the preen routine, but Gloria insisted. Her face was turning pale, her skin was drying, and even though we could barely notice, she knew it and hated it. She needed more time to meet her standards.

As the crowd waited, the mood lightened. Doug joked about Strauss time, in which every minute must take 100 seconds. A clock could not govern them, and if it tried, one of the children probably would break it. Anthony and Sam used the delay to amuse guests with their spunk, running through the packed room in their pajamas, chasing each other, bumping and stumbling along the way, giggling without cease.

When Gloria entered the room, the boys stopped their game and sat. She greeted her supporters, weary yet gracious. She took a seat between her parents on the couch and just above Maria, who rested on the hardwood floor, where she would soon fall asleep. Before the prayer session began, Doug whispered to Gloria, "What should we have for breakfast tomorrow?" His random mind made her chuckle, and now that there was levity, the supplication could begin.

Doug ran his hand through Gloria's hair and told us that one of his Kennedy High students would play an opening song, a piano instrumental she composed. Lisa Tran, a freshman, sat at the piano and performed a tender, nostalgic tune. The music felt like it pined for simpler times, a tribute to youthful exuberance. She called it "A Prayer for Gloria."

After Lisa finished, Doug declared, "We are here to glorify God through Gloria. No spectators allowed. Don't spectate. Participate."

Maybe I should vacate.

I didn't plan to pray; I was here to write about people praying. I am a reporter, and Ringman, my friend in the corner, is a photographer. We are journalists, newspapermen; we cannot pray on an assignment. It would be a conflict of interest. We might have to expose that Jesus turned water into wine without a liquor license.

Doug looked my way and gave a serious stare before winking. I nodded, put down my pen and placed my notebook on my thigh. At least I could close my eyes and let the experience flow through me.

First, they recited the rosary, Gloria's favorite prayer, and I mumbled along, a foreigner to most of the words. Gloria never felt pain during a rosary. It was her safe house, a place invisible to her foil of a disease.

It was a Wednesday, so they focused on the Glorious Mysteries: the Resurrection of Jesus Christ, the Ascension of Jesus to Heaven, the Descent of the Holy Ghost, the Assumption of the Blessed Virgin Mary into Heaven and the Coronation of the Blessed Virgin Mary, Queen of Heaven and Earth.

I felt so Catholic reading from my "How to Pray the Rosary" pamphlet.

The rosary began with the Apostles' Creed, the Our Father and the Glory be to the Father prayers, so it was manageable at first. Then, as they introduced each mystery, they lost me. There were a lot of Hail Marys, and then one person would speak and the group would respond, and this went on and on and on. I listened, peeked at my cheat sheet, listened some more, and at last, I caught the rhythm.

It sounded like a holy form of hip-hop.

When I say go, you say Jesus. Go! Jesus! Go! Jesus!

When I say Hail, you say Mary. Hail! Mary! Hail! Mary!

I listened to the crowd meditate on the Sacred Mysteries, and when I realized everyone was praying through Mary to reach Jesus, it stirred my spirit. Growing up Baptist, I always heard that Catholics defocused Jesus by using Mary so much. I never accepted that line of thinking. I thought it had traces of elitism or just pure ignorance, the kinds of attitudes that start religious wars. I chose to stray from group logic, but I had not revisited the topic until this night.

Here, it was clear. Forty people were doing everything in their humble hearts to enhance their relationship with God. How could Mary not be involved? It would be like a child visiting a friend and never acknowledging the mother. It would be rude, foolish, ignorant. For years, I had thought of prayer in such a myopic manner, so no wonder it was so hard even to kneel at bedside before I fell asleep. I had secluded myself from the spirit of prayer, making it a chore instead of an opportunity, choosing to tiptoe before God instead of approaching him confidently, hand-in-hand with as many worshippers as possible.

Holy Mary, Mother of God, pray for us sinners, now and at the hour of our death. Amen.

I was brushing the dust off my soul. This level of faith was still overwhelming to an outsider. After the rosary, a smaller group stayed for two more hours, and Tom Curran, the family friend who runs a Catholic ministry, led that session. Tom has a kind yet forceful presence about him. Tom grew up in Boston, so he has a bit of a New England accent, but he spoke in a whisperingly emphatic way. Even when he talked loudly, his voice was soft and nurturing. His tone made his points stick better than if he had used bombastic inflections.

Doug and Kristen met Tom around the time Gloria was born, but he didn't become a huge part of their lives until several years later, after Kristen was diagnosed with MS. From there, the relationship strengthened to an inseparable bond. Kristen befriended Tom's wife, Kari. When the Strausses learned Gloria was gravely ill, Tom began praying with them. Now, the Strausses considered him their spiritual mentor.

The late-night session wasn't just prayer; it was a full submission. An honest, wrenching conversation. It was open-heart religion. They spoke to God like they would a best friend after a breakup. I had never knelt before God in this manner.

* * *

My methods, in contrast, had resembled meeting the president. *Hi, Lord. Nice to meet you. You're doing a great job running, well, everything. You have my vote.* And then I would ask for what I wanted. Repent for sins without really going into detail (*Forgive me for whatever I did, the stuff that I remember and am too proud to admit and the stuff that I have forgotten because there are so many commandments.*) Ask for what I wanted again. Offer the obligatory thanks to God for being so good...you know, better than I've been to myself. Give a shout out to Jesus. Ask for what I wanted again. Amen.

I used to not be that terse, I think. It had been a while, though. As children, my brother and I were so attentive during worship at Lincoln Heights Missionary Baptist Church in Paducah, Kentucky, that we could recite everything said during a service. It was easy, actually, because people were redundant with their prayers.

Our favorite was Deacon Jones, a tall man with a bad back who spoke in a high-pitched voice. Deacon Jones always summoned God by saying, "Oh, Father! Oh, kind, Heavenly Father. Here we are, Father, a few of your poor, weak and humble servants have gathered this morning, Father. We didn't come for no shape, form or no fashion. Neither because we thought we kept thy commandments so well."

Then Deacon Jones would go through about two minutes of largely inaudible pleadings because his voice got higher the harder he prayed, but we knew to anticipate his finishing kick. Deacon Jones always ended with an abrupt close, a sign-off that came without any logical transition: "Until that day when we can't do anymore of thy service, amen."

It was like he talked to God until he ran out of breath and dove for the finish line. We loved Deacon Jones' consistency. We loved going to church, especially when the service concluded within two hours, hardly a certainty with the loquacious Reverend Alfred Anderson preaching.

So this night unleashed all my spiritual angst. It was invigorating.

During a pause in prayer, Doug looked at me and flexed. I laughed and closed my eyes, desperate for more of this warm feeling. Gloria napped throughout most of this second session, a side effect of painkillers. The rest of the children were already in bed. While Gloria slept, Mom stroked her hair, and Dad rested a hand on her shoulder. Eyes closed, heads bowed, they fought for their daughter until almost midnight.

Doug and Kristen pleaded for a reminder that Gloria was strong, that their six other kids could handle this burden, that they were using the right approach.

"We need a sign, Lord," Doug said, clenching his hands and tilting his head skyward. "We need a sign."

They took a break to carry Gloria into her bedroom, and after thirty more minutes of prayer, the session ended. As the prayer warriors left, Doug thanked me for joining them.

"I saw you over there," he said. "You weren't a spectator. You were feeling it."

I chuckled. I headed for my Escalade, feeling like I had been soothed while praying for Gloria. I wanted more of this elixir. I needed more. I was just the latest soul to realize it.

After the visitors left, Doug went to check on his daughter one last time. Gloria was awake when he entered the room. She apologized to her father for not having more energy. She admitted she was a little stubborn, too, apprehensive at the thought of another night before so many people. Dad hugged his daughter tight.

She rose from the bed and accompanied her father into the den. For the next few hours, she joked with her parents, suddenly spry, suddenly Gloria. She laughed and danced. She imitated the voices of all the judges on *American Idol*.

To end the night, she sang. She was practicing her favorite country number. When she hit the chorus, she burst with enthusiasm.

"I feel like a woman!"

CHAPTER FIVE

EXTREME MAKEOVER

The woman looked at Doug and Kristen with awe.

"You have glitter around you," she proclaimed.

Her statement confused the couple. The woman explained.

"That's a sign of holiness," she said. "When I see you in my mind, I see glitter. Tell me about yourself."

The woman's name was Margarita Pasos, and she stood next to her husband, Alejandro. They were visiting from Nicaragua in late April as special guests at the annual Kennedy High auction. They were invited by Lou Tice, a Kennedy graduate who helped found a Seattle-based enterprise called The Pacific Institute, which provided personal-motivation training for organizations around the world. A South American celebrity, Margarita hosted the talk show "Margarita te voy a Contar."

"Wanna go for a walk?" Doug asked Margarita and Alejandro.

The parents took Margarita and Alejandro to the Kennedy chapel and shared Gloria's story. They revealed their worries, their bold confidence in a miracle and their fears. When they were finished, Margarita told them to look down.

"There's glitter by your feet," she said.

This time, she was not speaking metaphorically. Doug and Kristen saw the small pieces sparkling beneath them.

It led the four of them into a discussion of the people who travel to Sarapiqui in Costa Rica on the first Tuesday of every month to witness the Virgin Mary appearing in the sky. At times, while gazing up at the vision, people have spoken of the sudden manifestation of glitter on their arms. They remembered a story about Our Lady of Guadalupe, an apparition of the Virgin Mary in sixteenth-century Mexico, when a man named Juan Diego followed the melody of sweet singing up a mountain until he found a superhuman woman shining atop a cliff speckled with glitter.

At the end of their conversation, Margarita left the parents with a message: "No matter what, trust in the Sacred Heart of Jesus."

The next day, Doug noticed an object gleaming in the fireplace at home. He picked it up with one finger and chuckled.

It was a little red heart.

* * *

Doug called to share his excitement, but I was too distracted to grasp what he meant. Ringman and I were lobbying our editors to get this story in the newspaper quickly. We feared Gloria might die soon. We also thought it was selfish to keep watching the tale develop while Gloria sank deeper into hopelessness. We knew Gloria would make for a powerful series, and we weren't ready to begin such a project, but we had to do something now. Perhaps someone would read it and know how to help Gloria. Perhaps others with strong faith would want to help the Strausses connect with God. Who knows? Our consciences told us to put a story in the paper immediately.

Our editors agreed. We decided the piece would be the main story in the Sunday sports section, even though it now had little to do with sports.

Ringman and I cared only about real estate; we would worry about the rest later. And who knew if there was time for the rest, anyway?

The story was to be about the daughter of a basketball coach struggling to lead his family, the family's uncanny faith and the titanic decision the Strausses needed to make about whether to continue with medicine. My challenge was to include just enough basketball to make it impersonate a sports story, but the key would be capturing Gloria's magnetism.

"If readers fall in love with Gloria, we can take this story anywhere," I told Ringman.

He nodded. Ringman was an understated guy, deft at deadpanning, but we had developed a good chemistry. We both believed in the power of Gloria's message and craved to depict its uniqueness. We knew it would be a battle to make others understand it, including those in our own office, and the obstacle sparked a mutual, defiant passion that would carry us through this journey.

To complete my reporting, I did a one-on-one interview with Gloria. We chatted for ninety minutes while her family members pressed their ears to the door. We talked about music, food and college. We covered go-kart riding, fights with Maria and prayer. We ventured into her stress over completing makeup work at school, her adamant desire for people not to see her as the girl with cancer and her intimate knowledge of her condition.

"I may not be good at math," Gloria said, "but other kids don't know neuroblastoma like I do."

Gloria was the oldest eleven-year-old ever. She was so mature, so perceptive. For all her fantasizing about stardom, for all the faith she put into a miracle, she was also realistic.

"Just hearing a timeline on my life, it scared me," she admitted. "I'm praying about trust. I still, every once in a while, start to cry when I think about things."

She worried mostly about her family members, about the strain put on them, about whether her siblings would feel unloved because of all the attention she gets. Her greatest concern was that her siblings would see her as spoiled.

"It breaks my heart," Gloria said. "I didn't ask for cancer. People are just being kind."

I thanked Gloria for spending time with me and told her she might be the best interview subject I have had in my career. She responded, "If there's a movie director reading, tell them she'd love to be...OK, just kidding."

My big story came out on Sunday, May 6. In the newspaper business, nothing compares to the reward of a Sunday centerpiece. The circulation on that day is nearly 400,000. The advertising makes for a robust product, which makes it a showcase for reporters, photographers, columnists, graphics specialists and page designers. If you have a great story, you want it in the Sunday paper.

On the front of the sports section, there was Ringman's beautiful picture of a prayer session at the Strauss house. It looked like a painting, with Gloria resting as her parents extended their arms toward her in prayer, with Joe and Maria sleeping in the foreground and with the community of prayer warriors bowing their heads in the background. The headline underneath the photo read, "A prayer for Gloria," a nod to Lisa Tran's beautiful music.

The readers loved Gloria. By midday, I had received a couple hundred e-mails and phone calls. People wanted to pray with Gloria or help the Strausses financially or share their own struggles with cancer. In addition, Doug and Kristen were surprised at the number of folks who looked up their number in the phonebook and called them directly.

"Thank you," Doug told me. "But who at *The Seattle Times* is going to come over here and answer our phone?"

That was the price of stardom, I told Doug.

"There is prayer on the front page of the sports section," Doug said. "Never thought I'd see that."

"It's who you are, right?" I replied.

"Absolutely, and we're not changing," Doug said. "Our faith is only getting stronger."

"Well, at our best, our goal in journalism is to portray the realness of life," I said. "As long as it's authentic and worthwhile to readers, we have a responsibility to tell those stories. Hey, I need to talk to you about where we go from here. And I need to talk more to your wife."

Doug invited me to visit again the next week, after the family returned from a mini-vacation in Ocean Shores, a getaway location on the Washington coast. A friend offered the Strausses a chance to stay at his condo, so Doug took a few days off and let his children skip school. The family needed to be together and isolated, both for quality time and for the privacy to make a decision on Gloria's cancer treatment.

The parents also learned how their children were truly dealing with the crisis. Maria longed for more attention, so her parents spent hours with their nine-year-old, resting in the bed, nourishing her with hugs and kisses. Joe seemed angry, so they calmed him, and later in the trip, he was urging the family to pray. Anthony wanted an audience to watch him goof, so they gave him an audience. Sam simply wanted to be Sam, free and reckless, running when he should be walking, so they let him exhaust his three-year-old energy, occasionally exclaiming, "Sam, throwing stuff is not OK to get our attention!"

It was an ideal three-day break. Gloria and Alissa played together like they did before illness and teenage freedom got in the way. The Strausses laughed and cried, watched movies, laughed some more and made sure everyone understood Gloria's predicament. They took turns holding baby Vincent. It was amazing to see how the six other children looked after Vincent, how they embraced him without jealousy. With seven kids, one would expect factions to develop, but it had yet to happen to the Strausses.

"I say it's easier with seven," Doug said. "Maybe I'm fooling myself, but that's what I say."

* * *

While the Strausses were away, their friends attempted a herculean act of generosity. For years, Gloria had wished her family could be on the "Extreme Makeover: Home Edition" television show. It never worked out, but their friends thought they could mimic that dream. So the clusters of Strauss supporters united for the first time. Parents, students and teachers from Kennedy High were there. Close friends from St. Philomena Catholic School, which the Strauss children attended, were there. Two Federal Way church families, St. Vincent de Paul and St. Theresa, were there.

About 75 volunteers gathered to do a complete renovation in three days. Some would stay through the night to make certain this project would be finished in time. They cleaned and painted the house, tidied the yard, hung framed pictures on the walls, installed fresh carpet and bought a new trampoline. Kelley Masterson, who met Kristen eight years ago when they were sponsoring people about to enter the Catholic Church, provided her artistic touch by personalizing the paint jobs in each bedroom. In Gloria's room, which she shared with Maria, Kelley made silver stars atop a pink background and inscribed "Glow" inside them.

I was amazed to see their effort. Some of these groups had just met each other, and yet they worked with great organization and chemistry. Why so much, I asked. Doing yard work and a few laundry loads would've been an incredible gesture, but this was the kindest act I had ever seen.

"We're giving our all out of love," Kelley said afterward. "It was amazing. I've never seen anything like that. Oh, you see it on TV, with people responding to natural disasters and other tragedies, but it's different when it's just between you and the clicker. Up close, it's hallowed ground. I can't believe we did so much work. God was transforming the ordinary to the extraordinary. Love is an action word. Love doesn't talk because talk is cheap."

I connected with Kelley immediately. She was one of the women who welcomed me into the Strauss house that first day. Kim Freyberg was the other, and her daughter, Taylor, was another of Gloria's best friends. All the women in the Strausses' lives are much like Kristen—kind, spiritual and loyal. Kelley was the most eloquent of the bunch, so expressive she could give a curmudgeon goose bumps.

When she was introduced to Kristen, Kelley fixated on the sweetness of her voice and thought, "Gosh, I like that girl." It didn't take much for them to become friends. They were part of the same women's spiritual group, so they saw each other at birthday parties, baptisms and Independence Day celebrations. Near the beginning of Gloria's cancer fight, Kristen and Kelley went on a women's retreat. The theme was "The Woman at the Well." Kristen exposed her heart during that getaway and mentioned the miracle in public for the first time.

Kelley came away thinking, "She knows where to go for her strength."

I asked Kelley if Kristen's testimony made her cry.

"I didn't cry," she replied. "Whenever you get a sense of God's presence and his perfect timing, in a moment like that, you just feel enkindled. You feel that warmth of His presence, and that excitement and anticipation that comes with it. Hope, that's what He shows you. Hope. It's weary, or it's jubilant. It can wax or wane. But a fervent hope feels like a party. Whatever your Father wants to give you is a jewel."

One chat with Kelley, and I almost caught up on all the church time I had missed. Kelley became a religious guide for me, especially when it concerned Catholicism. Whenever I needed to be uplifted or refocused, she offered nourishment, usually unsolicited.

"I've seen Kristen when she feels like her arms are tired from hanging on that rope," Kelley said. "But it's not very often. You look at her, look at Gloria, look at the entire family, and your cross shrinks."

Doug and Kristen referred to their helpers as "little angels," and it was becoming clear why there were so many. They were not seeking just to give. They were getting plenty in return.

Mary Caldwell, another family friend, explained it to me best: "When we pray for Gloria, it's like we're the ones receiving the blessings. We're receiving the healing. It's very humbling. It's been life-changing for all of us. But more than anything, we want to see Gloria full of life. It's a miracle already. But we want to see *her* miracle."

At least there were days that lowered the stress of this ambiguous quagmire, days such as May 10, when the Strausses cruised into the driveway of a refurbished home.

Doug noticed the trampoline first and then the yard, thoughtfully manicured right down to the placement of two-foot statues of Mary and St. Francis of Assisi. The children ran inside, screaming and squealing, finding surprises in every room. Alissa admired her new makeup station. The boys were wowed by the cars bearing their names painted on the walls. Doug and Kristen found new bed linens and a framed picture of them dancing at their wedding.

Gloria basked in the happiness. It was not the nationally televised home makeover she hoped for, but this was more meaningful. She knew her tribulations hindered the family's ability to function normally, from doing household chores to preparing dinner at night. Her parents tried hard to conceal the fact and make the abnormal seem typical, but Gloria was too astute at reading the situation and too compassionate to ignore it.

Trouble had stopped chasing the Strausses. For how long, they didn't know. They were at peace, however, even with the big decision looming. They floated through the rest of the night.

CHAPTER SIX

MS

From another room, Sam was making so much noise it was hard to determine whether he was injured, raging or jubilant. Kristen ditched her sweet talk for a firm demand.

"Sam, you have five seconds to come here!" she yelled.

After her son raced into the room, Kristen kissed him on the forehead and told him to quiet down.

"I love you," she said in conclusion.

Sam ran from the living room, back to where he could not be seen, and he stopped being a distraction for the rest of my visit.

"Kids thrive on a routine, and it's way out of whack now," Kristen said as she shook her head. "It's a tough balance."

Mom sat on the couch with a towel covering her while she nursed Vincent. Without question, it was the only interview I had ever done during a feeding. I smiled, squirming on the inside, focusing on her forehead in case the towel slipped. It took a while to relax. Fortunately, Kristen was adept at making any situation comfortable.

"I have a baby who's very clingy," Kristen explained, laughing. "I think he senses something is not quite right."

Kristen possessed an enchanting quality. She made people feel as if they were the most special person in her life. She was the prototypical affectionate mother. Doug loves to mention all the times he would awake in the middle of the night to the sound of Kristen smooching one of their children. With adults, she put them at ease with her kindness and managed to carve out time for substantive conversations. If Kristen had five minutes for you, it was the deepest five minutes possible, and most likely, it would spill over into fifteen minutes.

Problem was, her attentive nature left her with little privacy. I wondered how she made space to think and recharge. And then there was the MS issue, something Kristen tucked under her mellow temperament, a nonissue as long as she displayed a healthy and happy disposition.

She preferred not to talk about MS, especially with Gloria struggling. She hadn't felt its impact since overcoming her exacerbation in November 2002. She had willed it to footnote status, but the fear of another attack always lurked, and in the deserted corners of her being, the prospect haunted her.

To fight the disease, Kristen self-injected the drug Copaxone daily. She usually did it late at night, when the kids were asleep and the visitors were gone and the phone wasn't ringing. She pulled the medicine from the refrigerator, waited thirty minutes for it to reach room temperature, filled a syringe and jabbed the needle into her skin. The routine never got any easier, and her injection never came without a wince. But she had progressed, at least, from those days five years ago when she needed her husband to stick a needle the length of an ink pen into her thigh. Back then, Kristen would stare at a cross every time Doug jammed in that needle.

MS is a chronic disease that intensifies over time. It is a vile instigator, striving to make a body's immune system destroy its central nervous system. For Kristen, the symptoms appeared slowly and coincided with giving birth.

After Maria was born, her face went numb, but because the problem did not persist, she ignored it. Almost two years later, Kristen had Joe, her fourth child and the first boy. Doug's friends always joked he could not make boys, but he was proud to produce one after three girls. Six months later, Kristen's body started to malfunction.

While staying up late one night to fill out an application Alissa needed for school, Kristen was frightened to learn she "could not think my hands to write." She laughed. She joked she had a brain tumor.

"I know that's crazy to say, but at that point in my life, I was really at peace," she said.

She remembered a pivotal date, February, 28, 2001—Ash Wednesday. Kristen felt dizzy and numb, so she called her doctor. While she was on the phone, an earthquake shook the region. The kids curled under a table, and when it was over, they stood and looked at Mom for direction. Kristen was still dizzy.

"Is it done?" she asked. "Is the earthquake over?"

Alissa, who was seven at the time, looked puzzled.

"Yeah, Mom, it is," she replied.

Kristen visited her doctor but went home without an answer. The following Sunday night, Kristen was talking to Doug and fell, face first, without lifting her arms to brace herself during the collapse.

"We're going to the doctor," Doug said.

Doug carried her to the car, and at the hospital, an emergency MRI showed lesions on her brain.

"You have MS," the doctor told her.

Kristen was crushed, but she also obsessed over the name of the man examining her. He was Dr. Pope. "We thought that was significant," Kristen said, laughing.

Later, Kristen theorized her struggle was God's way of preparing the family for Gloria's cancer. Before that perspective came, however, she endured terror. Seizures blitzed her body. She tested medicines that gave her little relief. She even tried acupuncture and acupressure. Nothing worked. She grew depressed.

"It sounds silly, but I felt like I was totally consumed with me," Kristen said. "I was in bed, people were waiting on me, taking care of my kids, and I could do nothing but rest and wait for this thing to go away, calm down or do whatever it was going to do."

Her most frustrating moment came after a doctor advised her not to have any more children. Pregnancy is considered a security blanket for women with MS, as the body unites to protect the baby, but in the aftermath of birth, the symptoms escalate. Kristen reacted angrily.

"We'll see about that," she said. "What gifts children are to us!"

She switched doctors. Kristen always wanted to have a big family. As a child, she wrote in her diary about desiring fourteen children. Seven girls, seven boys. That was no longer the goal. Nevertheless, she and Doug were so open to life that they refused to accept limitations. Besides, the Catholic Church had ingrained its pro-life edicts in them.

Kristen returned to good health, got pregnant again and delivered her fifth child, Anthony, in early 2002. Several months later, MS pummeled her as expected.

I was astonished to learn how willingly Kristen sacrificed her health. Some would call it brave, others foolish. She called it love.

Her second exacerbation was equally rough, but she survived. Since then, she has had no major problems. She gave birth to Sam and Vincent without the MS symptoms ravaging her.

"I recently had an MRI, and I have a very healthy-looking brain," Kristen said. "The doctor said there's no doubt that my faith has helped me with my MS."

Right then, Gloria walked past us and went outside onto the deck. Kristen looked at her daughter carefully, inspecting every movement. Gloria was peppy, not even the slightest limp.

"Sometimes, I wonder, 'Is this God healing her right now?'" the mother said.

Then Kristen reasoned Gloria's pain medicine dosage was too high to be sure of anything. Dr. Park just upped it. Drugs inhabited her body every second of the day. Still, Kristen kept her unshakable trust in the miracle.

"I find myself just going through the day like it's a normal day," she said. "I don't think about death. I don't think about the possibility of Gloria dying. I assume she's going to be with us like all of our children are. I mean, we could get hit by a bus on the street and die. I just trust."

I scraped at her resolve. "All the time?" I asked. "Come on."

"Once in a blue moon, I have negative thoughts," she responded. "And when I start to think that, I don't dance around with the thought. I just jump back to where I was. I'm not going to go there. Some of the time, I would be like, 'Maybe I'm in denial.' But then God gave me scripture about the idea that there was going to be a miracle. I just feel like I'm in complete grace right now."

＊　＊　＊

If only I could say the same. Here was the great inconsistency in my life at the time: The more embedded I became with the Strausses, the less certain I was that there would even be another story. Ringman and I tried to leave that door open in our first piece, and even though it roused the interest of readers, our editors balked at continuing with a full-blown series.

My supervisor, the sports editor Cathy Henkel, had approved the project before exiting on a four-month leave of absence. Bill Reader, an easygoing assistant sports editor, took over her leadership role and backed the idea. However, once the top editors of the newspaper saw how detailed the series would be, they grew hesitant. Bill and I were asked to meet with Mike Stanton, an assistant managing editor.

"I'm not sure this can work," Stanton said.

I clenched my jaw. My heart fell to my pancreas. I wasn't sure whether I would need an ambulance or a punching bag.

My proposal detailed a seven-part series, explaining Gloria's dilemma and ending with the Strausses' big decision. I hoped an underlying question would frame the idea: How far are you willing to go for what you believe?

"If I pushed you out this window, Mike, would you trust that someone would catch you?" I asked. "That's what this family is trying to decide."

Word of caution: It isn't wise to mention pushing your boss out of a window. Fortunately, Stanton was a cool editor. During my job interview, I had so much fun chatting with him about the ideals of journalism. I could talk to him in an unrestrained manner. He didn't mince words, didn't watch his language, and he was guaranteed to challenge all of my points with his opposing viewpoint.

"I hate to play devil's advocate here," Stanton kept repeating.

It was a peculiar cliché considering the religious undertone of my project.

We argued and argued and argued. I was impressed with Bill's passion. He was usually so laid back. Although it became obvious to me that my proposal failed to capture the power of this tale, Bill comprehended it and believed in it.

"This is a story you have to feel," I pleaded to Stanton. "You can't just think it."

He countered that we would be setting readers up for a punch to the gut. I told him that our newspaper had already done enough gut-punching to win the heavyweight title.

"It's not our job to preconceive how people will feel about a story and not tell it because it would make them feel a certain way," I said. "Let's do what we always do. Let's tell the damn story clearly and objectively and have them decide."

Stanton asked if I thought Gloria would die.

"That's what the doctors say," I said. "The Strausses think otherwise. I believe in God, and maybe that helps me see their side of the story. But it's not about who I think will win. It's about how strongly they believe and how many people have joined them on this journey. South of Seattle, down in Federal Way, there's an amazing story going on. It shouldn't even be a question of whether to keep telling it."

Stanton countered that Ringman and I had told the story too thoroughly in our first piece.

"That's not even the tip of the iceberg," I said. "Think of that as the pilot episode. The people loved it. Now let's give them the full show."

Yes, but in the newspaper, it would be hard to work around that first story, he said.

"Look, we really like you," Stanton told me. "We don't want you to be upset at the paper this early. How long have you been here? Eight, nine months? Because you've done such quality work, we're willing to keep trying to figure out how to make this work."

I leaned forward and said unblinkingly, "This story will define my tenure at *The Seattle Times*."

Stanton had an idea. Maybe Jacqui Banaszynski could help. Jacqui was a former *Times* staffer who had become, in the minds of many, the best writing coach around. In 1988, while working for the St. Paul Pioneer Press in Minnesota, she won a Pulitzer Prize in feature writing for a penetrating series about AIDS, about two gay men and ultimately about life and death.

The series was titled "AIDS in the Heartland," and she wrote those pieces in a style refreshingly alternative to traditional journalism. She infused piercing insights and observation with raw compassion. She wrote like a human being struggling with a difficult story, not an exploitative journalist. I wanted my series to be a peer of hers. When Stanton mentioned bringing her in to rescue this project, I knew the doubts of upper management would soon dissolve.

The next day, Bill and I met with Jacqui, who had spent most of the night mulling possibilities. She uncovered a fantastic resolution. Instead of pitching a seven-part series that ended with this big decision, I needed to take the whole journey with Gloria. She asked if I could handle it. I nodded yes. She asked if the family would allow it. I told her probably.

"Make sure they understand exactly what this entails," Jacqui said. "Regardless of the outcome, they must be willing to let you and Steve walk with them. The door must always be open."

Jacqui also proposed I write an online journal about my emotions while covering the story.

"If you will do it, it's a kind of transparency that will attract readers," she advised. "You can build an online community while sitting vigil with Gloria."

Stanton accepted the recast series, and so did the bosses above him. Jacqui saved us. Now I had to back up my audacity and deliver tenure-defining work.

I was about to become more than a sports columnist. This series would run on the front page, so that meant I faced the task of writing for two different sections. Bill agreed to let me take days off from writing sports when necessary, but Steve, my columnist counterpart, had asked for a few months off for personal reasons, so Bill still needed me to come up with frequent columns. I would have to cover sports during the day and the Strausses at night. If the family was up for it, I had the energy and enthusiasm.

After thinking it over, Doug and Kristen said yes. The impact of that first story gave me credibility with them, and my frequent visits were like therapy sessions to them. Having a reporter around actually helped them be more open, a concept as new to me as interviewing a nursing mommy.

Re-energized, I listened to my recording of that conversation with Kristen. It lasted three hours; it felt like forty-five minutes. She rarely devoted that much time to sitting and talking. Doug always worried about her busy schedule and plotted how to create more leisure in her life.

Most of the time, it involved church. One night, after a stressful day, Kristen went to Mass alone. The congregation sang "On Eagles' Wings," a beautiful hymn about the virtues of trusting God.

And He will raise you up on eagles' wings,

Bear you on the breath of dawn,

Make you to shine like the sun,

And hold you in the palm of his hand.

Kristen called her husband on the drive home. Doug told her to take her time. He wanted her to walk through the door as mellow as possible.

When Kristen pulled into the driveway, she saw crows swarming over a tree. They were loud, alarmingly so. Kristen feared their next move, so she stayed in her van. She watched the crows fly over the house, make a circle and rush out of her sight. Still uncertain, Kristen remained in the van. The next time she looked up, she observed what riled the crows.

It was an eagle, as bald as Vincent. It flew a foot away from her windshield, seemingly in slow motion. Kristen could see it so clearly, right down to the crows pecking at its dark wings.

She wanted to grab hold and fly with the eagle. She knew it would shake the crows eventually. As she continued to watch, the eagle flew higher and higher, higher and higher, out of sight.

Gloria's confidence and sense of humor came from her father, Doug.
© Paul Dudley

CHAPTER SEVEN

JESSICA MORLEY

"Have we ever told you about the time Gloria fell out of the bleachers?" the parents asked during my next visit.

I shook my head no. Doug and Kristen smiled at each other and revisited the memory.

Gloria was three years old. Doug was coaching a basketball game. Kristen let her child wander away for a few seconds, and Gloria slipped through an opening in the railing and descended. She hit the ground with so much force that the sound of it stopped the game.

Kristen ran down from the bleachers. Doug sprinted from the bench. They were horrified, powerless, and in the ambulance, Doug could only promise Gloria ice cream once she got through the ordeal. It turned out she had a concussion, and she licked away her ice cream and her troubles that day.

"That's how we feel right now, like our daughter is falling," Kristen said. "Only this time, we're the ones dropping her, and we're certain God will catch her."

The decision had been made. No more cancer treatments. No more chemotherapy. No more experimental drugs. Goodbye, fenretinide, cefixime, irinotecan and temozolomide. They were test drugs that, in Gloria's desperate state, could only help her win a game of Scrabble. OK, Jesus, your move.

"I always knew it would come to this," Kristen said.

I billed it as a showdown. God versus cancer. Heard of the Thrilla in Manila? This was Bruising 'Em in Jerusalem.

It was a decision everyone expected. As the Strausses delayed their choice, their friends predicted they would not subject Gloria to more treatment. Doug kept referring to the zero percent success rate of the drugs Gloria was taking. Turning to God instead appeared to be this incredible gamble, but what other options did they have? If the Strausses had said they were abandoning treatment for Gloria to live out her final days, they would've been like thousands of suffering families. But their ebullient faith in a miracle created a perception that they were Bible-thumping risk-takers.

I struggled with how to portray the decision. Play it up too big, and Doug and Kristen would be considered negligent parents shunning smart doctors and chasing after holy ghosts. Downplay it, and the heart of this tale would be diminished because within the decision lay a moment of truth. It answered one essential life question that we all encounter at some point: Where to turn when there is nowhere to turn?

I went to Gloria for her insight. Her pain was ratcheting up, so much so that she couldn't attend school regularly. Her father took a leave from work so that Gloria could have both of her parents around all the time. She would act normal for a few hours and then fall asleep abruptly, a side effect of her pain medication. I wanted to know what she hoped people comprehended when they thought about her.

"I hope people get that it's going to be a miracle, and I'm going to make it," she said. "A lot of the time, people will cry and go, 'I really hope.' I know for a fact I'm going to make it. I'm really sure about that."

"But we are so programmed to be cynical, Gloria," I replied.

"I feel like people, through this whole thing, have been inspired by me," she said. "I know some people who have almost become Catholic because of this."

"And what about the people who love you but can't think the way you do because they're so scared to lose you?" I asked.

"Maybe if people are worried for me or afraid, I really want them to pray about it and think to themselves, 'She's an amazing young girl, and I don't see why on Earth she'd leave.'"

She captivated me once more. Glow proved true to her nickname. She shined, even in darkness. She did it with her own special drama.

*   *   *

To test my perception of Gloria, I delved deeper into her past. I wanted to know what people outside of her family, close friends and faith community thought of her. I wound up learning about the impact she had at the American Cancer Society's Camp Goodtimes.

After being diagnosed with neuroblastoma, Gloria became a regular at Camp Goodtimes, a free summer camp for cancer survivors and kids still in treatment. Each camper was allowed to bring one sibling, and two years ago, Gloria brought Maria. Each cabin was required to create a skit or lip synch routine and perform it in front of the entire camp.

Sonja Korum, the volunteer who looked after Gloria's cabin, watched as Gloria and Maria taught the rest of the kids a dance and cheer song called "Tootie Tot." All week, laughter erupted in the cabin late at night as the sisters stood with their feet apart, knees together, arms out, thumbs up, butt out and tongue out as they sang the song. Sonja, whom the kids called Ducky because all the older camp helpers were tagged with playful aliases, will never forget the routine.

A tootie tot, a tootie tot, a tootie tot ta
A tootie tot, a tootie tot, a tootie tot ta
  Arms out!
A tootie tot, a tootie tot, a tootie tot ta
A tootie tot, a tootie tot, a tootie tot ta
  Thumbs up!
A tootie tot, a tootie tot, a tootie tot ta
A tootie tot, a tootie tot, a tootie tot ta
  Feet apart!
A tootie tot, a tootie tot, a tootie tot ta
A tootie tot, a tootie tot, a tootie tot ta
  Knees together!
A tootie tot, a tootie tot, a tootie tot ta
A tootie tot, a tootie tot, a tootie tot ta
  Butt out!
A tootie tot, a tootie tot, a tootie tot ta
A tootie tot, a tootie tot, a tootie tot ta
  Tongue out!
A tootie tot, a tootie tot, a tootie tot ta
A tootie tot, a tootie tot, a tootie tot ta
  Turn around!

All the girls in the cabin practiced the routine over and over, amused every time. One night, Ducky looked over and saw Gloria off to the side doing the cheer by herself. She was in front of a bathroom mirror, making sure her movements were precise.

"Tootie Tot" stole the show. The girls wore princess crowns while they performed, and afterward they called a few staffers up to join them. There was so much joy in the room, especially at the sight of Gloria and Maria working so hard to keep the staffers from missing steps. That year, the girls were asked to dance again during the parents program on the last day of camp. Ducky looked around her and saw most of the staff grooving along. Since then, "Tootie Tot" has become a fixture at Camp Goodtimes. In all that she did, Gloria was memorable.

*　*　*

During my Camp Goodtimes research, the name Jessica Morley kept coming up.

"Who's Jessica Morley?" I asked Alissa one afternoon.

"She's one reason we have hope for Gloria," Alissa said.

Jessica survived neuroblastoma as a child. Doctors diagnosed it when she was eleven months old, zapped the disease with radiation and chemotherapy, operated on her, and the cancer went into remission after a year and a half of treatment. The only remnant was a side effect known as Horner's syndrome.

Jessica met the Strausses when she was in the eighth grade. Her school required a service project, so she decided to help the family. When she knocked on their door, a short-haired Gloria opened it, flashed the brightest smile and escorted Jessica into the house. Gloria's enthusiasm dazzled Jessica, but she really didn't get close to the family until the next year. As a freshman at Kennedy, she befriended Doug, and later he put her to work, baby-sitting and running errands.

Because of Gloria, Jessica came to understand the ruthless disease she once had. She was fortunate doctors found her cancer early. Although the situations were vastly different, the Strausses still looked at Jessica as a sign that neuroblastoma didn't have to equal death.

Jessica resisted the role-model tag. She was more interested in what Gloria had given her.

"Just meeting Gloria has made me blessed to realize the healings I received," she said. "There's really nothing I want more than for her to be healed."

One of Jessica's good friends at Kennedy, Theresa Brennan, also became one of Doug's helpers. They seemed like twins, both so humble and generous and grounded in Catholicism. Theresa grew closer to Gloria during baby-sitting assignments, when Glow would con her into staying up as late as she could. Back then, Gloria had to take a handful of huge chemo pills before bed. She swallowed each one slowly, hoping to stay up and talk. Theresa would become enthralled by the things Gloria said—goofy one sentence, sage the next—and lose track of time.

"Gloria, you have to take another pill," Theresa would demand.

"No, no," Gloria replied. "I gotta wait ten minutes."

Theresa was a face among the masses to me until I received an e-mail from her. After the series resumed and moved to the coveted real estate of Page A1, and after my online journal debuted, Theresa wrote to say that, during the first prayer meeting I attended, she was skeptical about the presence of a reporter.

"Does he really know what we're doing here?" she wrote. "Does he really get it?"

My writing was winning her over, however. In my first journal entry, I answered the question of whether I thought Gloria would die. I talked about my faith, my hiatus from church, my fascination with the realness of the Strausses and my challenge to write the series in a manner that resonated with the godly, the agnostic and the atheist factions.

Theresa appreciated my candor and urged me to write from the heart. She shared her tussle with faith, with being the best Catholic she could be while transitioning toward adulthood. She didn't write from her seventeen-year-old mind. She sounded like my grandmothers, both in their seventies, who frequently tried to probe my relationship with God.

"Did you go to church today?" Grandma Hightower would ask.

"Remember to keep your eye focused on Jesus," Grandma Brewer would say.

If I took her words literally, it meant I could focus my other eye on something else, like football. Or women. There were so many distractions, and my mind was too jumbled. Embarrassed to say, but if those Come to Jesus pep talks got too heavy, I hung up and claimed I lost my cell signal. By the time we reconnected, my grandmothers would've changed topics.

Sometimes, it takes a fresh voice to re-create an old message. Theresa did that for me in her e-mail. I felt pride and motivation when I finished reading it. I thanked her and promised to rummage my soul for perspective, even while striving for objectivity.

At the same time, I had long acknowledged one thing my journalism peers were reluctant to admit: the idea of pure neutrality is an utter fallacy. Only a robot could muster that level of indifference. As journalists, our mission is not to delete our humanity. It is to control it and channel it into great storytelling. If that weren't true, newspapers would neither care about diversifying the newsroom nor possessing the skill of news judgment. Every story would be an unfocused cluster of conflict, with no sense of good or bad, right or wrong, substance or fluff.

That isn't our objective. We have the responsibility to gather the best information available, use our intelligence to decipher it and present it to readers based on our understanding of the situation. All stories require reporters and editors to take a leap of faith. Our objectivity begins with our sincere motivations and ends with a thoughtful consideration of all opposing viewpoints. Readers would always try to judge objectivity on whether they agreed with the message, but as long as we approached journalism properly, we could be the bearer of all flavors of news.

* * *

Finally, I called Dr. Park to get her opinions on Gloria and her reaction to the Strausses' decision to stop cancer treatment. She was an impressive doctor, tough yet tender, with a passion both for getting to know children and for curing their illnesses.

"Sometimes, this is a sad business," Dr. Park admitted. "Gloria is special, like all the children. She's quite mature. She talks about her disease in a rather developmentally advanced way. She's very unique in that way."

During visits with Dr. Park, Gloria was famous for asking the majority of the questions, sometimes thirty or forty of them. Dr. Park admired her strength and the source of that strength. She didn't shun the family's faith, but she spoke honestly about the dilemma.

"From your view, with all the miracle talk they speak, are the Strausses still being realistic about Gloria?" I asked her.

"I have no intention to take away their hope for a miracle or how they believe a miracle will come about," she replied. "I think my job is to make sure they're grounded. And they are. Every family of a child dealing with an illness wants a miracle. Others don't have it as crystallized as this one."

Dr. Park respected their decision to stop cancer treatment. She still had ideas on solutions. She never ran out of ideas. Dr. Park became interested in specializing in childhood cancer during medical school. She wanted to be a general pediatrician until she realized the obstacles that cancer-stricken children faced and the advances in research that needed to be made.

Her job was one of the toughest in medicine. It often meant losing these children. It often meant using, well, breakdowns as an opportunity for a breakthrough.

"Kids, they don't want to be sick," Dr. Park said. "They don't want to act sick. They don't want to look sick. It helps us keep our focus in the right place. We are very humbled by how far we have to go to cure all the kids."

With Gloria, the task was now to keep her comfortable as the cancer attacked. Dr. Park fought for her patients until the end.

"There's still a lot I can do for her," she vowed.

Pain was the biggest obstacle. She wanted to monitor Gloria's pain closely, for it would be the greatest indicator of the cancer's activity.

When Doug and Kristen told Dr. Park of their decision, they were worried she would be upset. Kristen hawed while speaking, but the doctor interrupted her.

"You're not just doing nothing," she said. "You're doing something. I know that."

The three shared tears, some for trepidation, some for expectation, all for Gloria.

PART II

ROSARY

Christmas 2003 in Indiana. Front (left to right): Maria, Anthony, Kristen, Gloria, Grandpa Clem Miller, Alissa, Alex Trimberger, Joey Trimberger. Back (left to right): Vicki Trimberger, Doug (holding Sam), Joe, Danny Trimberger, Pat Trimberger and Paul Trimberger. Photo courtesy of the Strauss family

CHAPTER EIGHT

THE SLOW LIFE IN INDIANA

F or all her star talk, Gloria dreamed simpler, too. She was not a princess; she only pretended to be one. Her primary goal in life: to enjoy her family. If fame was unattainable, she had a backup plan.

"I'd want to go to Indiana with my family and have kind of, you know, a slow life," she said.

Her maternal grandparents lived in Mishawaka, Indiana, a suburb of South Bend, home of the University of Notre Dame. To the Strauss children, it was a mystical place far, far away, a town containing the roots of their faith.

"The slow life in Indiana, huh?" I asked Gloria.

"My family and I are always bragging about South Bend, Indiana, because we have so much family out there that even spreads the news to their friends," Gloria replied. "It's kind of like there's prayer *everywhere.*"

For the Memorial Day weekend, the Strausses flew to Indiana. A friend of Pat and Vicki Trimberger, Kristen's parents, donated the use of a private jet, and the nine Strausses loaded into the plane, whereupon they laughed at the location of the ninth seat. It was the toilet, and it even came with a seat belt. The kids haggled over who had dibs.

When they landed, Alissa made a call from her mother's phone and learned she was elected as the hospitality commissioner for the next school year at St. Philomena. Alissa, who was about to be an eighth-grader, had given her speech in front of the entire student body before they left, reinventing the Mickey Mouse theme song.

Who's the leader of the pack
It's plain for you to see
A-L-I-S-S-A
For hospitality!

Gloria, Maria and Joe helped their sister perform. They all wore mouse ears, entertaining the crowd to cement Alissa as the most unforgettable candidate. With the momentum of her victory, the trip was bound to be a success.

Pat and Vicki resided in a neighborhood full of family. The streets should've been named after all the members of the clan, just to keep track of everyone. Bridget lived two doors down, and across the street was her mother, Bev, one of Vicki's ten siblings. Bethy, another of Bev's daughters, lived a block away, and across the street from her was Michael. Within a mile, there was Betsy, Louie, Jennifer and Mary Claire. And those were just the ones who immediately came to mind.

"We're all over this place," Vicki said.

They were praying for Gloria, too. Pat and Vicki hosted a rosary during the visit, and the Strausses were awed by all the people who were gathering regularly to call on God to help Gloria. The house was packed, just like it was in Federal Way. Suddenly, the distance of two thousand miles seemed a lot closer.

The standard of Clement and Mary Louise Miller reigned here. Vicki's parents were the perfect mix of spirituality, humor and love. They knew how to live. They used to delight in taking long drives—the Oldsmobile

Treatment, they called it—afternoon cruises that slowed life to the speed of their car, enabling their minds to stay fresh. Their love story began the day Mary Lou saw Clement hanging in a tree with his buddy, which prompted Mary Lou to point at the friend and tell her cousin, "You can have that. I want this one."

Clement and Mary Lou were married in 1937 and didn't part until her death sixty years later. They had eleven children: Mike, Bev, Brian, Mary Beth, Hub, Wayne, Joyce, Ginni, Vicki, Greg and Alicia. They were tough parents without being mean. The kids were more afraid to disappoint them than make them angry. Clement used to threaten them with the Cold Water Cure. He told them he would take a cold washcloth and wash their faces.

The kids nicknamed their parents Mary Lou Censor and Clem Curfew, allusions to how they governed the family. Mary Lou played the piano; Clem made furniture. He could do almost anything, from remodeling houses to fixing engines to making rosaries. A Notre Dame sports fan, Clement used blue beads and gold crosses to create his rosaries, and he gave them to friends and family members as gifts.

After she gave birth to Alicia, her eleventh child, Mary Lou decided she was done with doctors. She would pray novenas and hope for good health. When she reached her eighties, she started having problems. She finally returned to a hospital, and the visit didn't go well. Lung cancer. Mary Lou never smoked, but she had lung cancer. Later, doctors told her she had brain cancer.

On a Wednesday afternoon, Vicki went to her parents' house, ready for some Oldsmobile Treatment, but Mom had changed. She had a glazed look. Vicki got in the car and shared a petrified look with her sister, Ginni.

By Friday, Mary Lou was in a coma. She died the next day, September 27, 1997.

Her passing was a wonderfully cleansing affair, however. About sixty people came to the house, singing and praying the rosary. The television was tuned to the football game, family members brought food, and kids played in the yard. The family was disturbed over how much Mary Lou suffered in her final days. She looked like a woman in labor at times, but at the end, serenity ruled.

"It was like God gave her a choice: Die and go to Heaven immediately or do redemptive suffering," Vicki said. "She chose redemptive suffering."

Clement was lonely, but he managed. He moved into a different house with his daughter Bev, whom he referred to as his Hafta-Hafta-Gotta-Gotta Girl. He endured major buyer's remorse over the new house at first, fearing he left his wife behind, but eventually he would like it enough to call it a "good little house."

He wasn't the most articulate man. However, his words stayed with his family, especially his pet phrase, "Rock-A-Socky." It meant a number of things. Right on. Go get 'em. Hang in there. Stay strong.

Go to Clem with a problem, and he would say, "It'll be OK. It'll be OK. Rock-A-Socky, it'll be OK."

At ninety years old, he still drove himself to Mass. He also climbed onto the roof and cleaned the gutters. Family members would drive by, see his ladder out and tell him not to think about doing the chore. Clem smiled.

"Oh yeah, oh yeah, oh yeah," he said. "I'm just gonna sit here. I'm just gonna sit here."

Five minutes after they left, he would be on the roof.

Clem died of cancer in October 2006. His last days were even more powerful than his wife's, as he praised God with newfound eloquence while his relatives sat vigil. His words were so pure and joyous that his family began jotting down everything he said. Every close relative received a copy of the transcription. At the Strauss house, Grandpa Miller's death-bed incantations rested atop the piano.

"Jesus, you are sweet," he said. "I love you. You are the Great One. You are the Great One. Again and again, we thank you. Jesus, Jesus, talk to me, Jesus. Jesus, help. Jesus, be kind. Jesus! I love you in the morning,

Jesus. I love you in the evening, Jesus. Jesus forever! My Lord is a gem. I love Jesus Christ."

At one point, Clement exclaimed, "Jesus! Jesus! He's our man!" So the family followed up with, "If he can't do it, no one can!"

It was a pleasurably sad time.

"You are the Strong Guy," Clement said. "We praise your name even against opposition. Clear the road. Clear everything! Tell me what you want. Lord, what do you want to say?"

Vicki dabbed her eyes as she recalled how her parents exited.

"You really sensed that you were in the presence of angels," she said.

*   *   *

Gloria represented the best of her great-grandparents. As her relatives gathered for a barbecue, she disguised her rising pain to have a good time. Everyone wanted to hug her, kiss her, talk to her, and she obliged until she grew too weary to mask the aches. She would fall asleep often, leaving the family to fret once more about the severity of her condition.

At the barbecue, John Miller, one of Kristen's first cousins, told Doug he had quit smoking because of Gloria. John handed him a St. Philomena prayer card and mentioned how much praying to the saint helped him find the strength to toss aside cigarettes after thirty years. Doug turned white.

"Are you OK?" John asked.

"The school Gloria goes to is called St. Philomena," Doug replied.

They refused to accept it as coincidence. The relics of Philomena were brought to her school once, and Gloria held them, so they took that as another sign. They were amazed at another uncanny connection involving Gloria.

Philomena gained saint status solely because of the astonishing intercessory moments she has provided. Pope Gregory XVI beatified her in 1837 and named her the Patroness of the Living Rosary and the Patroness of the Children of Mary. Or the Wonder Worker, for short.

In 1802, the bones of a young girl, roughly fourteen, were discovered in Rome, in the catacomb of Saint Pricilla on the Via Salaria. An inscription near the tomb read: "Peace be with thee, Philomena." There were also a glass vial of dried blood and drawings of a palm, two anchors and three arrows. Based on these symbols, Philomena was dubbed a virgin and a martyr.

Three years later, Father Francis Lucia of Mugnano, Italy, became overwhelmed with a sense of joy while inside the Vatican Treasury of Relics. He asked if he could take Philomena's relics home to enshrine them in his chapel. He thought the relics could lift the spirits of his parishioners, just as they had for him.

After he enshrined those relics, miracles occurred. People were healed of incurable ailments, the most famous being the Venerable Pauline Jaricot, who made a pilgrimage to Philomena's tomb. Pope Gregory XVI admired Pauline greatly and was on hand to see her healed of heart disease by Philomena's bones, and he was so moved that he began the process of making Philomena a saint.

While Doug and John explored St. Philomena's significance, the feeling of a miracle grew stronger. Gloria and St. Philomena? Gloria and the Wonder Worker? United? There had to be something to it. This had to be a sign.

*   *   *

The best part of the trip was yet to come, however. Kristen wanted to be in Indiana on Memorial Day weekend because her new favorite author, Immaculée Ilibagiza, was in town speaking at the National Medjugorje Conference. Vicki gave Kristen the book "Left To Tell: Discovering God Amidst The Rwandan Holocaust," and she read it during Gloria's hospital stays in February and March. The riveting memoir touched all of Kristen's emotions. She pictured what Immaculée described: a young woman hiding in the bathroom of a pastor's house for ninety-one days while killers with machetes hunted for her, begging for mercy as the bloody genocide continued, developing a deep relationship with God. Her bond with God was so everlasting that Immaculée forgave the savage men who killed most of her family.

Kristen was on fire about Immaculée. She wanted to meet and hug her. When she entered the Joyce Center at Notre Dame, where Immaculée was speaking, Kristen started to cry. After Immaculée delivered a message of unconditional love, the Strausses and their relatives wandered backstage. They hoped for any kind of acknowledgment from Immaculée. A smile, a hello, anything. They stood in a hallway, waiting for her to emerge from an interview room, and when she exited and began walking away from them, she noticed Vincent and stopped.

"I need to hold the baby," Immaculée said.

Kristen cried again.

"Can I hug you?" Kristen asked.

"Immaculée, this is our daughter, Gloria," Doug said. "She has cancer."

Immaculée comforted Gloria and said, "You pray the rosary, don't you?" Gloria smiled.

"You continue to turn to the Blessed Mother," Immaculée told her. "You will be a miracle."

Then Immaculée handed Gloria her rosary and walked away.

"Well, that was better than a book signing," Kristen marveled.

Still, Gloria ached. When she had nothing to make her laugh, she gave anguished looks. She sat on the couch with her grandmother and requested Vicki tickle her arms.

"I know I could die," Gloria said to Grandma. "I don't want to die, but I know if I die, it's God's will."

Vicki held Gloria tightly, absorbing some of the girl's strength. Gloria only feared how her family would respond if she died.

At the end of the trip, the family awoke to an uplifting sight. Gloria had energy again. And no pain. She went outside, and as Pat and Vicki looked out the window, they saw their granddaughter, giving Sam a piggyback ride, walking toward Grandpa Miller's old house.

"Where are you going?" Vicki asked.

Gloria twisted around and gave her answer.

"I want to smell Grandpa's clothes."

CHAPTER NINE

TRAVELING NURSE

Steve Ringman called with an update.

"Hey, Jerry, it's Ring," he began.

Our relationship had progressed to abbreviated handles. We were tight.

"I was with Gloria today," he said. "She's not doing too good."

"More pain?" I asked.

"Yeah," Steve replied. "And the Strausses started talking about hospice this morning."

My mind reverted to another of Gloria's dreams. Beyond being a celebrity and a family anchor, she wanted to impact the world with her heart, to grind her strife into the antidote for victimized people around the world.

"I've always wanted to help people," she said. "Be a nurse and travel to natural disasters like the tsunami."

Gloria was referring to the 2004 tsunami that ravaged Thailand. Back then, she wept as she watched the news on television.

"Is that how many people died?" she would ask her parents whenever the screen flashed the death toll.

When her parents nodded, she fell silent.

After Hurricane Katrina tormented the Gulf Coast in 2005, Gloria demanded, "We have to pray for these people."

Awareness wasn't good enough for Gloria. Caring wasn't good enough. She always needed to do something, and there was no doubt she would make a fine traveling nurse.

Now, in a cruel twist, she would soon have hospice nurses traveling to see her every day.

"It was hard to watch, Jerry," Steve said. "She gets exhausted so easily because of the pain pills she's taking. One minute, she's like normal. The next, she's in a deep sleep."

It was mid-June. It had been two months since Dr. Park gave the dire prognosis. Gloria was popping twenty-four pills a day for pain, a cocktail of Tylenol, Advil and methadone.

My next visit verified what Steve had said. The methadone made Gloria itch, and her arms turned red from scratching. Once, Doug and Kristen were late serving Gloria her meds, causing the pain to rush through her body, and they became frighteningly aware of the cancer's destruction. It bombarded her, and she cried uncontrollably. If the medicine didn't stay above Gloria's pain level, it took hours to ease her discomfort. Mom and Dad couldn't be late, not even a half-hour tardy, or they risked being defenseless as Gloria writhed in agony.

"That's why hospice might be the right thing to do," Doug said.

He looked haggard. He wasn't sleeping. He thought he had pneumonia but refused to go to the doctor.

"You should tell him how bad he looks," Kristen whispered to me. "Maybe he will listen to you."

"Are you OK, Doug?" I asked.

He shook his head and walked to the bedroom for a nap.

Doug's parents, Steve and Diane Strauss, started visiting more frequently. Diane was a dynamo, capable of handling any task that eased a burden. Sometimes, she watched the other kids. Sometimes, she did household chores. On this day, she sat on the couch and let Gloria fall asleep in her lap.

Gloria trusted her grandmother's touch. She was vulnerable around Grandma, for she knew Diane understood her obstacles. Grandma survived breast cancer. She treated it like a gnat, swatted it away and laughed whenever someone called her brave.

While she was sick on chemotherapy, Diane demanded she get to continue baby-sitting her grandkids, and she seldom missed watching Doug coach his basketball games. She drove herself to pneumonia, rested and drove even harder.

Diane received her final chemo treatment the same day Gloria had her first. They sported bald heads at the same time and took a picture together, an image Grandma cherished.

Gloria had seen Diane lose her hair before. The first time Grandma was bald, her hair came back gray.

"Grandma, I don't care what color my hair comes back as long as it's not gray," Gloria declared back then.

Grandma chuckled.

"I actually feel I got cancer so I could help Gloria through her cancer," Diane told me.

She admitted, however, that it was getting harder to help. The Strausses had gone to see "West Side Story" at Seattle's 5th Avenue Theatre a few days earlier. A friend gave them backstage passes, but the catch was that their seats were split into two sections. Near the intermission, Kristen sent Doug a text message: "Gloria needs more pain medicine."

Doug rushed to the car. Diane took Gloria to the restroom during the break. At the theater, the bathrooms were downstairs, and on the way back up, Gloria couldn't bear the climb. She pressed down on Grandma's right shoulder, so hard that Diane asked if Gloria should wait for her father to come back and carry her. Gloria hated the idea, so she pressed and winced, pressed and winced, until they reached the theater lobby.

Driving home alone later that night, Diane cried.

The next time she saw Gloria, she returned to her upbeat attitude.

"Like everybody else, I'll have my moments," Diane said. "At work, I'll get to talking about Gloria, and then I'll say, 'We have to change the subject. I can't talk anymore.' If we all sat around crying and moping, what's going to do for her?"

"Nothing good," I guessed.

"I believe Gloria is going to have her miracle," Diane replied quickly. "Oh my gosh, we're filling the Heavens with prayer."

Diane is a small woman with a big laugh who has a great feel for when to push and pull back. The ability to listen is her greatest asset. She's willing to suspend her own emotions to be a sounding board for everyone in the family. She let Doug and Kristen vent to her, sometimes about each other, without repeating anything they said. She treated Alissa like an adult and gave her the same privilege to shout her frustrations.

"You learn a lot if you just keep your mouth shut," Diane said. "They have to be able to talk. They have to be able to get things out. As far as money, I can't help them with money, and with what they need, money's not going to help them anyway. So I give them all my love."

In return, they gave Diane their faith. Her husband was raised Catholic, but Steve Strauss, a wheelchair-bound former paratrooper for the 82nd Airborne Division, strayed from the church. After Doug found religion and started dating Kristen, Diane would "just listen to that girl talk about God and get inspired." Later, Diane became Catholic.

As Diane charted her unlikely path to holiness, she expressed surprise that her family had come so far. She and her husband lived in White Center, a low-income, high-crime area plopped between Seattle and Burien, where keeping the kids out of trouble was an accomplishment of biblical proportions.

"When I became Catholic, that just made Doug's world," Diane said. "Doug has really come around in life, I'll tell you that. We all have. You couldn't ask for better people, I don't think."

The family still bickered, and no argument was louder than a recent one between Gloria and Maria over their room. Forget the pain. Gloria was a neat freak, and she thought her little sister wasn't doing her part. So Gloria cleaned the room, tidying up just the way she wanted. But Maria had one huge problem: Gloria seized her jewelry box.

Gloria's items filled the pink-and-white box, which sent little sis into a fury. Their quarrel rumbled through the house. Doug and Kristen tried to stop it, Alissa tried to stop it, but no one could interrupt this dispute.

"It's my jewelry box," Maria said. "You have no right."

"But you're not using it," Gloria said. "What's the big deal?"

Back and forth, they squabbled. As it progressed, the parents giggled. They were girls no matter what, debilitating cancer trauma one minute, petty antagonism the next.

A day later, it was ancient history. I asked Maria about the disagreement while she was coloring, and she brushed it off.

"It's great sharing a room with her," Maria said. "She's my best friend. It's fun, but sometimes it's complicated."

"Is it just the room that makes things complicated?" I asked.

"No, I get jealous because of all the attention she gets," Maria admitted. "A lot of times, I get left behind because I don't stand up for myself and stuff."

"Does Gloria know you feel this way?" I asked.

"Yeah, and she's really good about caring about how I feel," Maria replied. "She tells me she hates all the gifts she gets because it's not fair to the rest of us. She gave me some sunglasses somebody gave her. Her having cancer is kinda making her life miserable. When she loses the cancer, I think it's gonna bring a specialer life to us."

Maria, also a blonde, resembles Gloria. When people mistook her for

Gloria, she grew frustrated, but Doug and Kristen showed Maria photos that emphasized her unique features and bragged about her inability to take a bad picture. While Gloria wanted to be an entertainer, Maria was the artistic gem of the family. When she finished coloring her bird, she walked me from the kitchen table to the front door. She wanted to show me one of her favorite drawings.

On the wall, Maria pointed to her interpretation of Gloria's miracle. In it, Gloria was dressed in a pink shirt with "Glow" written across it. She wore a yellow skirt with boots, and flying above her was an angel.

"She's a ballerina angel," Maria said. "I wound up giving her some shoes. I don't know why. It just came to me. Usually, angels don't have shoes on."

* * *

It was my last visit before the Strausses called hospice. They had no choice. They needed help keeping Gloria comfortable. It meant they had to think about the logistics of death, and thus began a tug-of-war between medicine and spirituality. The Strausses would acknowledge all possibilities, but they abstained from focusing on impending doom. They just needed to stretch time. God was coming; they could still feel it. God was coming.

"Have I told you about Kari Mannikko?" Doug asked. "You have to hear about Kari Mannikko."

Kari was a believer who had every reason to doubt. Neuroblastoma killed her son, Brandon, eight years ago. The wickedness of the disease continued to terrorize her, the way it probed Brandon's body until it spotted an opening and feasted mercilessly, a slithering illness that saved its nasty worst for last.

The end was intolerable. Kari applied a moist swab to his mouth when she peered down his throat to see what she believed were tumors. She held her little boy, only four years old, and urged him, "If you feel God calling you, it's OK."

Two nights later, after Kari observed a change in Brandon's breathing, she asked her husband, Brian, to call in at work in the morning. They stayed awake the rest of the night, placed Brandon across their laps and cuddled him until he died.

"I used to think of this disease like the ocean," Kari said. "It's quiet, and then big, roaring waves come, and your feet are sucked out from underneath you in a heartbeat. We try to get our minds around it, but it's so much bigger than what we know."

Yet she believed Gloria would be different.

"I don't think this is where her road's going to end," Kari said. "I don't think this is her time. I know what the prognosis is. I've been there. But I don't think this is it."

Kari, a friend from St. Vincent de Paul church, came to all of the prayer meetings. She was hesitant to share Brandon's entire story with the Strausses at first, and the Strausses were nervous about going there, too. They didn't want to hear about the perils. When they realized Kari had different insights, they were astounded.

She observed the differences as much as the similarities. Kari admired how open the Strausses were to having outsiders involved. The atmosphere, the holiness, almost muted the fear. And Gloria...Kari couldn't get over Gloria.

"I was there once when she prayed for her parents," Kari said. "I marveled at how incredibly wise she was. Children, they have such incredible wisdom, and you wonder where that comes from. It's a gift, a blessing. They understand better than us, and we've lived longer."

"Why do you believe so much in Gloria when you endured what Brandon went through?" I asked.

"I don't have the words for it," Kari said. "It's just a feeling that I have to go with. It's just faith. We have to believe. If we don't believe, we're giving in. I'm not saying we're being naïve and taking the sunny side, or that if you pretend it's not going to happen, then it's not going to happen. You're not going to know until that hour. Hope. If we don't have that hope, we give up. And if we give up, we're not helping anybody."

* * *

Upon finishing the interview with Kari, I called Doug.

"That Kari Mannikko—wow!" I exclaimed.

"I told you," he said. "And there's more where that came from. It's unbelievable how many people pray for Gloria. She's the most prayed-for child in the world. I'm telling you, it's true. Can you research that?"

"That'd be a tough one, Doug," I replied.

"Ah, c'mon, man!" Doug shouted back. "I thought you were a big-time reporter."

"I'm not that good."

"Oh, but you are good. I hear ya trying to be humble. You're good, but you're not that good. OK, I got it."

"So, what other Kari Mannikkos are out there?"

"Did I tell you about the blind man?"

Walter Bain was a part of the St. Philomena parish. Susan Roettjer, a friend of Kristen's, kept speaking of this sweet old man in his eighties who prayed for Gloria. He wanted to meet her, and one afternoon about two years earlier, Susan, Kristen and Gloria went to visit him.

Walter is legally blind. When they arrived at his house, he was reading scripture on the computer. He had taken off his thick glasses, so his face was nearly pressed against the screen. He was stunned as he looked up to greet Gloria.

He could see her clearly.

Walter didn't see the child in her blue-and-white school uniform, however. He saw her dressed in all white, looking radiant. Gloria prayed with Walter and blessed his rosary. When she left, so did Walter's sight.

Later, he wrote a letter to the family describing his experience.

"God was kind enough to do me a favor and return my eyesight to me long enough to see Gloria in all her beauty," he wrote. "She was truly beautiful. As she walked out the door, my blindness returned to me. She appeared to me dressed in all white, but as she left, she was re-clothed in her school uniform. My ability to see was taken away from me again."

After gathering all the information, I called Doug again.

"You can't just call them Kari Mannikkos anymore, can you?" he said. "There are so many stories like that. It blows my mind."

"You're right. I don't know what to say."

"Gloria's a healer. She makes your spirit healthy."

"It's truly amazing, Doug. I've never covered a story quite like this."

"My Geezy Deezy is at it again."

CHAPTER TEN

STRAUSS HOME VIDEOS

A prescription for Prozac lay on the kitchen counter. When Doug whisked by it to go check on Gloria, it skimmed the surface like a fallen leaf breezing across a lawn. Upon his return, the prescription made a U-turn, following a father trying to evade his troubles.

"Last night, I got up to look at her," Doug said. "She looked like she was in pain in the bed. I was talking to my friend, Mike. He told me to focus on God's will instead of what's happening. But her anxiety level is higher, and we increased her pain medicine again. Definitely, it's been hard."

I said nothing.

"It's been really rough," Kristen said. "When the pain intensifies like this, the doctors kind of have to play around with the medicine a little bit to see what works. With that comes frustration. Gloria is feeling frustrated and angry. And she's tired. She gets emotional about things. When she feels out of control, she gets angry. That's her way of being in control."

I stared at the parents, smiled meekly and asked, "Do you really think you're going to need to fill that prescription?"

They said nothing.

This was a side of the Strausses I hadn't seen. They were mystified. Gloria stayed in her bedroom the entire day, because the pain and the attention were too much. Everything was too much. She needed to sulk for once rather than be the sublime sufferer. She didn't want to talk or laugh or even keep her room neat. Mom and Dad cleaned her room, arranged her clothes and bargained with Gloria to compensate them with some cheerfulness. No. Gloria had little to offer.

After four years, the cancer spread to the most unimaginable place: her psyche.

Hospice brought her a wheelchair, but Gloria wouldn't use it, except for playing games with her brothers. Steve showed me a beautiful, intentionally-blurred photo he took of her holding Vincent as Anthony pushed her around on the deck. She looked solemn in the picture, unconcerned over the possibility of a wreck, caring only to give one brother the thrill of whirling her in the silly thing and the other a kind of coziness she also craved.

Gloria loved babies. They kept her sane. Since being diagnosed with cancer, she had welcomed Sam and Vincent into the family, holding them in between treatments, finding hope in their purity. When Doug and Kristen met criticism about growing their family during Gloria's illness, they watched their daughter rejoice in the company of a new life and cast their disapprovers as uninformed.

Most mornings, Gloria would awaken, grab Vincent and carry him around while she began her day, but her sore legs were robbing her of the pleasure. So the parents ushered Vincent to her, and Gloria rose from bed to kiss him, and then he was taken away as her struggle continued.

The Strausses were forced to suspend their large prayer sessions. A smaller group still came to the house regularly, and Tom Curran led them in deep, late-night entreaties. The rest of the community put together a worship schedule to continue supporting the family from afar: Monday night at the D'Angelos' home, Tuesday at the Currans', Wednesday at the Fantozzis', Thursday at the Brennans', Friday at the Caldwells'.

"Our community won't let us fail," Doug said.

* * *

My favorite person in their community was Jennifer Vertetis, Kristen's lifelong friend. Jen and Lori Rosellini, the mother of Gloria's good friend, Lexie, were sisters. Their maiden name was McCann, and the McCanns went way back with Kristen's parents, the Trimbergers, who lived in the Puget Sound region before moving to Indiana.

Pat Trimberger and Jack McCann built houses together. When their wives met, Mary McCann handed Vicki Trimberger a loaf of bread, peanut butter and jelly and said, "Make some sandwiches and pass them back." Mary was whom Kristen would become, a mother of seven scrambling through each day. Vicki was whom Jen would become, a mother of three.

It was poetic for the dynamic of these friendships to flip between generations, and the McCann/Trimberger connection was set to continue with all the children of Kristen, Jen and Lori interacting.

"I feel like Jen and Lori are the sisters I didn't have," said Kristen, who has two brothers, Paul and Danny. "Our children are like cousins to each other. It's great."

In the summers, the three families gathered at the home of Jack and Mary McCann in Kent, Washington, and the kids played in the pool while the adults talked. Lori always knew how to throw something fun in the direction of Doug and Kristen to keep the mood light. Jen was quick to provide junk food or make plans for a girls' night out. Both sisters were great at handling any problem Kristen had, providing a solution before she even requested help.

Jen was among the first people in the community to actively help me tell Gloria's story. The tale was so touchy—examining faith, chronicling Gloria's deterioration, balancing my desire for access with the family's need for privacy—that I expected resistance, especially from the Strausses' friends. If need be, I was prepared to stitch a scarlet R (for reporter) on my clothing. Catholics and the mass media weren't on friendly terms because of the reporting of sexual abuse cases involving priests, but this group was either more approachable than a village of companion dogs, or they had mastered quiet opposition.

Jen understood me from the start. She offered suggestions on how to best cover the Strausses and informed me of the things I missed. If Doug and Kristen were too busy to answer a question, I called Jen. If I was fishing for a fresh anecdote, I called Jen. As the president of a philanthropic organization, she relates well to everyone, and on top of being media-savvy, she's blessed with an innate genuineness that draws people to her. The petite brunette smiles constantly, yet she's tough. She's assertive, forceful when required, and she sees the big picture in any situation. Reporters always gravitate to the Jens of society.

Jen is married to a lawyer, Tom Vertetis, and they had two children at the time: Peter and Mary. Peter has autism, and Jen recalled one night in May when the adults were up late praying together. Their focus shifted from Gloria to Peter, from the Strausses to the Vertetises, and as they wept and pleaded to God, Gloria shuffled into the room.

She cuddled next to Jen, rested her head on her hand and quietly joined the worship. Jen didn't open her eyes until the end of the prayer session, but she already knew it was Gloria. She felt it. The child's compassion left an imprint.

"Here's this little girl, in more pain than anyone knows, in total peace, praying for me," Jen said. "It was the most beautiful thing."

To help her friends, Jen wanted to copy Doug's family videos onto DVDs. So Kristen put the camcorder and library of tapes into the family van one afternoon, anticipating she would visit Jen after spending some time with Alissa. Kristen sensed her daughter needed the spotlight, and she had a great idea: an escape to Wild Waves amusement park in Federal Way. She found a sitter for the other children, swept Alissa away and parked on the street outside of the park.

After enjoying some water therapy, Kristen called Doug as she walked back to the car with her daughter.

"Ohmigosh!" she exclaimed.

"What's wrong?" Doug wondered.

"Our car's been broken into."

Alissa noticed her purse had been stolen, including her iPod, camera, house key and favorite lip gloss. Kristen lost money, gas cards, gift cards and a breast pump.

"Who steals a breast pump?!" she shouted in disgust.

"Relax," Doug said. "It'll be OK."

At 10 that night, Doug gazed upon a beautiful moon. It had the illusion of a silver ring encircling it. It was an image he had never seen, an exotic, lunar Saturn floating in the air. He ran to grab his video camera and realized it was gone, too.

He burst into tears. Years of precious moments were lost: Gloria's cancer journey and most her life, the silly acts of all the kids, the night those rays flowed from the Virgin Mary statuette to Gloria.

"I was so proud of those videos," Doug said, shaking his head. "So proud."

The Strausses suddenly realized the severity and risk of the theft. The thief knew their address and had Alissa's key. What if someone raided their house? Should they stay elsewhere for the night? They argued, father versus mother, father versus children, mother versus children, pouting, crying, screaming.

"Why's this stuff got to keep happening to us?" several of the kids grumbled. "Haven't we had enough?"

Doug yelled over the noise.

"Let's say a prayer!"

They sat together and asked God to soothe them and remind them of the essential pleasures that no one could steal. They had their love. They had their happiness. They relaxed and left to spend the night at the McCanns' house.

During their retreat, Doug received a call from Margarita. As he explained the latest drama, she interrupted with a message.

"You know what you still have, though, Doug?" she asked.

"What?"

"The Sacred Heart of Jesus."

"Awww, Margarita, that's not what I want to hear."

"You still have the most valuable possession of all."

"Why do people always have to tell me the right stuff? I wanted to throw a pity party."

*   *   *

Although the Strausses found perspective, the theft had damaged their resolve greatly. Doubt surfaced, not about the miracle, but whether they would be able to handle the turbulence as they waited on God. They developed a wild hope that they could catch the thief, even without the help of a Federal Way police department that had bigger concerns, or encourage the criminal to show some heart and at least return the videos.

It was as if they needed this undercard miracle as a sign the main event was coming. At the same time, their urgency suggested panic that they had lost an irreplaceable portion of a life whittling away. They wouldn't admit it, couldn't admit it, but the robbery forced them to consider the void Gloria's death might create.

Doug played detective, and when that didn't work, he asked if I could write about the crime.

"I can put it in my online journal, sure," I told him.

"No, no. I think we need a story in the newspaper," he replied. "Maybe the thief will read it and be sad about what he did and return the videos."

"I'm definitely going to include it in the next part of the series."

"Yeah, but when's that gonna run?"

We'd been producing new stories for the series every two or three weeks. Despite all the reservations about how Seattle—generally regarded as unchurched—would receive it, the community had fallen for Gloria.

Still, I couldn't just write a random news story about the robbery, even though I wanted to, because the newspaper doesn't devote much space to petty thefts. We were already doing an in-depth series on the family. A big headline about their stolen items would be considered overkill.

"I'll ask my bosses, but I'm not sure it will work out, Doug," I said.

"Well, at least you're trying," he replied softly.

It killed me to disappoint him. So I stepped back for a few days and kept up with the family by phone and text messages. They needed a week with some space; I needed a week with some space. A delicate balance existed with this kind of reporting. As the reporter, I wanted to blend in as much as possible, wanted the Strausses to feel comfortable around me, wanted them to consider me an extension of the family. As a human being, the access made me ache with them, and that was dangerous. I had to restrain those emotions every time I sat at the computer, or else the tears would drown the words. I had to remember, as much as I cared for and admired these people, they were an assignment.

During our break, another media outlet learned of the stolen videos and interviewed the family about it. KOMO, the local ABC television affiliate, did the piece, breaking it down to its heartbreaking essence: Family of dying girl loses videos of her during happier, healthier times.

"It's not like I can be three all over again," Gloria said during the interview.

She was different. She was angry, dejected. She was tired of being an easy target.

Her parents tried to talk Gloria into attending a prayer session at the Fantozzis' house, but she shook her head. No. Gloria had little to offer, still.

"It's never been like this before," Kristen said. "It's always been hard, but it's never been like this."

Gloria's mood changed after a church friend visited, though. Debbie Kovach came to the house to serve Gloria the Eucharist. As they partook in it, Kovach asked, "Gloria, would you bless me?"

Gloria began crying. The moment and the request nudged her back into the right mindset.

She touched Debbie and prayed. "Lord, I'm sorry," the child said. "You know I've been down. You know me. Forgive me."

Doug and Kristen knew then that they could tear up the Prozac prescription.

* * *

Steve Ringman always wore a white button-down shirt when he visited Gloria. He must've had a walk-in closet full of them.

"Why don't you try to wear something else?" Gloria teased him. "Why don't you stop wearing the same thing over and over?"

Gloria critiqued everyone's clothing. You had to be careful around the little fashionista. I did my best to make my style a nonissue, but Steve was consistently blah to Gloria.

Then one day, he visited wearing a black button-down shirt.

"Hey, you're not wearing your white shirt!" Gloria exclaimed.

She beamed with pride. At last, her needling resulted in change.

He wasn't the only one catching grief. Doug acknowledged the big, white Escalade in the driveway.

"I've been meaning to ask you about your car," he said. "What, you been rapping?"

"Nah," I said, laughing to control my nerves.

This was the conversation I dreaded.

"They must pay you well at the paper," he said. "Can you get me a job?"

"What can you write?"

"Enough to get an Escalade."

I mumbled, most inaudible, something about the car being a nice "Welcome to Seattle" gift. In actuality, it was more of an impulse buy. I had a decent chunk of money saved, the fruits of being frugal for years, and when that dissatisfaction started welling inside of me, I tried to purchase some bliss. Didn't work. Foolish decision. This vehicle didn't uplift me; it actually lowered my self-esteem because it was such a misfit. I tricked myself into believing in a material myth. Call it liar's remorse.

"See you later, man," I told Doug, rushing to jump inside my ride and zoom away from the embarrassment.

"Bye, LeBron!"

On the drive home, I thought about wealth. I was doing all right, and the Strausses needed to plan in advance just to go to a restaurant. Yet I envied them. They had something more valuable. Their willpower was elastic. They withstood all challenges, and I labored to extinguish a sadness that wasn't even identifiable.

As that juxtaposition of morale became clear to me, I laughed, laughed so hard my cheeks got sore and my eyes got wet, laughed so hard I could barely control the steering wheel.

I was delirious. What an absurd depression I'd carried for months.

I remembered what Jen once told me about visiting the Strauss house: "When you walk into that house, you believe. You have to believe. In this miracle, in everything. I don't know what it is. You see all these beautiful kids and that beautiful girl, and you have to believe."

I called my family—parents, both sets of grandparents, brother—and explained the remarkable change I was experiencing through Gloria. We talked about the true meaning of happiness, about how to love the right way and, of course, about the relentlessness of a pure faith.

My family would grow to care about Gloria as much as I did. They checked in to see how she was doing, put her on their prayer lists and urged me to "hold onto God's unchanging hand," an oft-recited saying in our household. And they knew the message was being received again.

That night, I knelt alone and prayed for Gloria, ignoring time and chores and distractions. It was my first sincere, private prayer in a long time.

CHAPTER ELEVEN

THE BURNING BUSH

The aroma of ribs reached my nostrils before I opened the car door. Doug stood on his deck, grilling and blasting music. The CD player alternated between Motown classics and gospel music, mostly, and the father hummed along, grinning and expressing pride in his taste.

"Getting married and having three girls first, it changed my whole view of being a male and how to treat women," he said. "It changed my musical tastes. That's the first thing I always tell my students, 'Yeah, I was like you guys, listening to some of the music you listen to. Then I had my daughter, and then I realized the stuff that's being said in those songs.' I saw the faces of my daughters and my wife when I heard those songs again. When you've got a wife and three girls at home, you just can't listen to certain songs like...like...well, I better not even say. Gloria's in the house. She might come out and hear me."

I laughed. Doug was just warming up.

"I'm an old-school fan. The song from The Spinners...how's that go?" he asked.

He thought for a minute and started singing.

"Early one Sunday morning. Breakfast was on the table."

"You know what I'm talkin' about?" Doug asked. "What's the name of that song?"

"It's called 'Sadie,' I believe."

"Yes, that's it. They could've named that 'Kristen.' I tell her, 'There's not too many like you.' And then I start up that 'early one Sunday morning,' and I say, 'This is your song.'"

Doug didn't sing it as well as The Spinners, but it was nice to see him in good spirits. Only he and Gloria were home, so even with the music up, there was a stillness to the Strauss house. I had come to share some of the letters and e-mails that continued to fill my mailbox and inbox about Gloria. Once a week, I tried to make a mail-run visit just to keep the pile from accumulating too much.

Gloria was already the star she aspired to be, only she didn't realize it. She saw her growing popularity as people being compassionate or needing a faith boost, never pausing to think there was something about her that charmed the masses.

"I mean, I think I can make people laugh and stuff," Gloria said, "and maybe they see that I'm being tough or whatever. But like I said before, I don't really want to be looked at as the girl with cancer."

"I don't think people see you that way, Gloria," I said.

"You can never be sure."

I went to my car and fetched my laptop. I wanted to show Gloria that her charisma—not the cancer—drew the crowd. In early June, I had recorded a "Gloria: In Her Own Words" audio piece for the newspaper's Web site. The month was almost over, and she hadn't heard what she produced that day.

"Do you remember when we recorded that, Gloria?" I asked.

"Yes," she said, laughing. "The first time, you let me keep talking for twenty-one minutes, and then you told me you only needed seven!"

"And then you did it all by yourself, and it was perfect," I replied.

"OK, let's hear it," she said.

I cued the audio, recalling that day. We taped it in her brothers' bedroom. It was messy and smelled like boys, so we opened a window and flies buzzed about, sending me into a swatting frenzy. But Gloria was relaxed and focused. In the first two takes, I asked her questions about her family, illness and aspirations, but on the third take, she decided to do the interview by herself, without my questions. I left the room, and when I returned ten minutes later to review the tape, I listened to the voice of a wise and confident woman talking as if Barbara Walters were sitting across from her.

As we reviewed the audio, I told Gloria her words made one of the paper's web producers cry.

"Really?" Gloria asked.

"Yeah, really," I said. "Listen to the loving way you talk about your family and friends. Listen to the enthusiasm when you talk about your hopes and dreams and your faith. And then, after all that, you know so much about your disease. It's amazing."

"I sound like a little girl," Gloria replied.

"Oh, Gloria," I said. "Nobody likes the sound of their voice on tape. It's weird listening to yourself, ya know?"

"I still sound like a little girl."

I shook my head and grinned. Gloria put her hand on my shoulder.

"Here," she said, placing a bag in front of me. "Want a cookie?"

*   *   *

Less than an hour later, Gloria had vanished to her room and fallen into another deep sleep. I asked Doug if she was on the same pain medication.

"No, we're onto a mix of methadone and oxycodone now," he said. "The doctors keep trying and trying different things, but her leg's still hurting. She went to a pain patch last week, but that didn't work. So they gave her two pain patches, and that didn't work, either. So now we're here. When she's good, she's good. But when she's bad..."

He didn't need to say anymore. I didn't need to hear anymore.

"So, how do you make your ribs?" I asked.

Doug had several plastic bags of ribs steeped in a special sauce scattered throughout the kitchen. He paid extra attention to marinating the ribs properly, he said, and when they were done, he promised they'd be unlike any I'd tasted.

"I like to cook," he said. "I can cook anything. I like being Mr. Mom."

"Let me be the judge."

He handed me a rib straight off the grill. I sampled it, grinned and teased that he couldn't compete with my father or grandfather.

"Aww, man, they're not even here!" Doug shouted. "Where are you from again? Arkansas?"

"Kentucky," I huffed. "Where's your wife? She's a lot nicer."

Doug gave a victorious giggle. He always razzed me with his Kentucky disregard.

He walked into the living room and sifted through some CDs.

"Have you ever heard the Gloria song?" he asked.

"She has her own song?"

"Oh yeah. You've gotta hear this."

Doug found the CD, which he called "She Da Bomb," and recalled its origins before he played it.

A fellow Kennedy teacher, Joanne Lawrence, told him about a year ago that a nonprofit organization, the Songs of Love Foundation, composed personalized music for ill children. So he wrote a letter to the foundation, describing Gloria's illness, personality and family. Within days, Songs of Love had sent a CD in the mail.

It sounded like a cheesy, 1980s-style number, but it was catchy. It wedged Gloria's life into three heartfelt minutes.

She's da bomb
She's got it going on
Glor-eee-uh!
Glor-eee-uh!
Woo-hoo!
She'll win your heart
Right from the start
Glor-eee-uh!
Glor-eee-uh!
Woo-hoo!

During the three verses, Doug bobbed his head and explained the meaning of each. The first verse was about how much love Gloria has within her and her ability to captivate people with her faith. The second verse was about her style and unselfishness.

"I like this part," Doug said, anticipating the chance to belt out a few lyrics.

You'll want to snuggle with her!

The third verse was about her family. At the time, there were six children with, as the singer cooed, *another baby duuuuuue.*

"Oh, here comes my favorite part!" Doug exclaimed near the end.

Geezy!

Deezy!

"That's her nickname, remember? Geezy Deezy. My lil' Geezy Deezy. She'll bounce back. She always does."

He played the song once more, playing the music louder, singing along this time. During the chorus, he rocked back his head, looked to the Heavens and shouted, "Glor-eee-uh! Glor-eee-uh! Woo-hoo!"

* * *

The Strausses spent the Fourth of July at the McCann house. They were with the Rosellini family, which guaranteed a zany time.

Adam and Lori Rosellini had four children that matched up nicely with the Strausses' seven. Their three girls—Caitlyn, Lexie and Lindsey—

were ages fourteen, ten and eight, respectively, making it seem as if Kristen and Lori staggered the births of their daughters. Adam and Lori also had a twelve-year-old, Jack, who was six years older than any of the Strauss boys. Put the two families together, and eleven kids were born within thirteen years.

They treated each other like first cousins. And there were natural pairings within the group: Alissa and Caitlyn, the oldest daughters; Gloria and Lexie, the middle daughters; and Maria and Lindsey, the youngest daughters.

Amid the Independence Day celebration, Kristen surprised Doug with a plan she'd made with Lori.

"We're going to take all the girls and go to Lake Chelan this weekend," Kristen said. "I'll take Vincent, but it's you and the boys for a couple of days."

Although Doug wanted to be with Gloria as much as possible, he liked the idea. It was a mini-vacation, a chance for his daughter to get away from the cancer, in a sense, and do something adventurous. Doug and Kristen had debated for several weeks whether to defy their money situation and plan a major family trip—maybe New York, maybe Hawaii—so that Gloria could experience something new. Finding joy, even if they had to manufacture it, was their primary mission. Their Ocean Shores and Indiana excursions showed them how much the family needed to keep a fresh outlook.

This day wound up fitting into that category, too. When the evening hours began, it turned into a pool party with fireworks. Jack and Mary McCann, Lori's parents, owned a beautiful home in Kent, Washington, designed and remodeled by Kristen's father, with a pool area with a picturesque view of the Kent Valley. All family members and friends wanted to have their parties there, and Jack and Mary often obliged. They had accumulated wealth in their lives, but at heart they remained parents scrambling to raise seven children. They enjoyed the commotion of a busy house.

On this night, as the children scampered through the estate with sparklers, a bush caught fire. Alissa and Caitlyn saw it first, watching the action as they talked in an upstairs room. They ran to the pool area, screaming.

"Ohmigosh, the bush is on fire!"

Lori grabbed a hose. Doug picked up a cup and scooped some water from the pool. Adam looked at Doug, hustling toward the bush with a cup, and laughed. The others observed the goofy scene and joined Adam. So Doug splashed Adam with his cup of water.

Later, after the fire was out, the jokes continued.

"Oh, we just saw the burning bush," Kristen said, laughing hysterically.

"How biblical," Lori replied.

*   *   *

It took about three hours for the ladies, along with Jack McCann, to drive to Lake Chelan, a central Washington state recess locale nestled in the North Cascades. The lake itself stretches fifty-five miles long, blue and pristine, a boater's fantasy. At nearly fifteen-hundred feet deep, Lake Chelan is the third deepest in the United States (behind Crater and Tahoe) and the twenty-fourth deepest in the world. Adventure beckoned. The kids couldn't wait to go inner-tubing.

Gloria was feeling worse, however. She tried to disguise it, but everyone knew. She fell asleep in the van on the drive over, dozing off during the kind of party-like atmosphere she was used to creating. True to her nature, Gloria stayed chipper for as long as she could, which only made it more jarring when her body crashed.

After they arrived at Lake Chelan, Gloria's legs ached so much she couldn't walk up and down stairs. With her body failing her and her spirits sinking, she concentrated on doing her best to keep pace with the other kids. Somehow, she rallied yet again.

When it was time to go inner-tubing, Kristen and the others feared Gloria was too ill to participate or even ride on the boat, but there she was on a hot summer day, atop a tube tethered to the watercraft. Jack drove slowly, careful not to aggravate those aches. Gloria signaled for him to go faster. He declined and continued cruising, amazed at her resiliency.

"She just wants to live life to the fullest," Jack said.

Seeing Gloria so happy and peaceful on the water reminded the adults of fun times at the McCann pool. There was one particularly memorable occasion. About a year ago, when Gloria first learned her cancer was active again, doctors informed her that she'd need to have a medical port placed under her skin once more, which Gloria despised. But she found an upside: She had a chance to swim before the port was reattached.

Gloria and Lexie planned a sleepover at the McCann house, with Gloria convincing her mother, in dramatic fashion, to allow her to go.

She ran into the bedroom and declared, "Mom, it's a miracle!"

Kristen sat up and listened.

"Lexie just called and invited me to spend the night," Gloria explained. "I don't have my port in yet, so I can swim. Isn't that a miracle she invited me before I had to get my port in?"

Gloria smirked as she talked. She didn't attempt to hide her slick performance. Kristen called Lori, who agreed the sleepover was a good idea and offered to pick up Gloria.

"Oh, so you will come get her?" Kristen asked aloud.

"No," Gloria interrupted. "I already called Adam. He's going to pick me up on his way home from work."

That night, Adam and Lori sat on the deck, watching their four children and Gloria run, giggle and splash in the pool. They played Follow the Leader off the diving board, squirted each other with a cold water hose and warmed up in the hot tub. Adam and Lori sat in the distance, sharing no words, tears dripping down their cheeks.

Gloria was their goofy, funny, loud, loving friend. She made the best of every situation. When she couldn't swim anymore because of the port, she sheathed herself in Saran Wrap and dipped into the pool.

Of course, Gloria mustered the strength to go inner-tubing.

As the sun beamed down on the girls, Gloria rested on her tube and smiled through her pain.

"Oh, it's like a moving tan," she said.

* * *

With the ladies away, Doug took the boys to visit his parents in White Center. I met them a few hours later, and Doug played tour guide in his old neighborhood.

We walked several blocks as he recalled his adolescence. The area was a cultural melting pot, an unincorporated, impoverished village that seemed a prime candidate for gentrification whenever rich people could get around to caring.

"You might want to watch your Escalade around here," Doug joked. "Hope you have full coverage."

He pointed to a Walgreens store about a hundred yards from his parents' home.

"That used to be a Chubby and Tubby store," he said. "If I ever get money, I'm going to buy that lot and build a house. And I'm going to name my house Chubby and Tubby's."

"Chubby and...what was that again?" I asked.

"Aww, c'mon, man!" Doug exclaimed. "You don't know about Chubby and Tubby's? I keep forgetting you're new to this area. Guess they don't have 'em in Arkansas."

"Kentucky!"

"Aww, my bad."

I thought to myself about where I'd be without Doug and his family. Even though I didn't know the area, I was beginning to love it, and they were a big reason for my happiness. I had regained a balanced perspective. I enjoyed being in public, whereas before I generally stayed home when I wasn't working. I met a new woman, Karen, but after so much disappointment in the love department, I was hesitant to accelerate that relationship too soon. Luckily, she was patient with my slow pace.

Despite my trepidation, there was no doubt I wanted what Doug and Kristen had. Watching them together for the past three months had redefined the standard of a loving couple. My parents had been married for twenty-five years, and both sets of grandparents had surpassed fifty, but it was different watching a couple so close to my age.

Many nights, while driving back to my apartment from the Strauss house, I thought about the Doug and Kristen love story. It was so pure, so them. It was imperfect, yet their pursuit of righteousness was charming enough to offset their flaws.

They graduated from Kennedy in June 1992. On January 23, 1994, they had their first child, Alissa. However, they didn't marry until six months later, and in that half year, they altered their lifestyle.

Back then, they were nineteen-year-olds living together with a child on the way, not exactly textbook Christian living. Doug proposed to Kristen the Christmas before Alissa was born, and that's when family and friends started coaxing them to make a sacrifice and live in a more church-approved manner.

They persuaded Doug and Kristen to live apart until their wedding. The couple referred to it as an opportunity to "start over." Kristen moved back in with her parents. Doug remained at their apartment nearby. He visited Kristen and Alissa every day, but he always returned to his place at the end of the night. Doug and Kristen were also abstinent during those months.

"It was the best thing we ever did," Kristen said.

"We wanted to be able to tell our children this story when they got older," Doug said. "It's never too late to do the right thing. We wanted to enter our marriage the right way."

Thirteen years later, their relationship was only getting better. Doug took me to a White Center coffee shop and excused himself temporarily to swap text messages with his wife. Unsolicited, he revealed his key to a good marriage.

"We're first in our family," he said. "We're Number One."

"Really?" I asked.

"If we're happy, it's a byproduct that our kids will be. The rest falls into place. It's a trickle-down effect. A lot of people focus on their kids, but forget about their marriage."

"So, you try your best not to neglect Kristen?"

"It's more than that. We know that we have to make the time to go out together. If you don't, you can go months without spending quality time together. We love our kids. We spend as much time as we can with them. But when it's time for Mommy and Daddy to be alone, we have to be alone."

"I see, I see."

"We've had seven kids, so you know we've created some alone time."

I nearly spit out my vanilla latte before laughing so hard the barista stared at me. Right then, another text from Kristen popped into Doug's cell phone.

"Gloria isn't feeling any better," Doug said, sighing. "We really need to get her home."

On the return trip from Lake Chelan, Gloria's pain rose another excruciating level. In the van, she cried and cried. The respite had ended. The fun was over. The persistence of these tears, harsher than ever, indicated as much.

CHAPTER TWELVE

DEN

In the family den, Gloria lay on her back, crippled by cancer. She couldn't walk; the pain made her legs feel as if they were trapped under bricks. The aches were spreading, too. She talked of soreness in her arms, and though cancer doesn't quite work this way, it felt like the evil was rising from toe to head.

Hospice brought Gloria a hospital bed shortly after she returned from Lake Chelan so that it would be easier for her to adjust her body position. Her medicine changed again, to morphine and then to Dilaudid. An IV sent thirty-five milligrams per hour of Dilaudid into her body, and if she remained uncomfortable, she could press a button every eight minutes to shoot twenty more milligrams into her system. Even so, these painkillers couldn't help her get out of that bed.

So Gloria dreamed of a better life. She dreamed of her old life, of being able to go to the bathroom without assistance, of dancing and performing.

It seemed so real that she fooled herself into believing it was true. She awoke in the middle of the night, giddy. She tried to rise from bed. She shifted to the edge, legs dangling, ready to restore her vitality. Then she paused as reality rushed through her. Pain, again. Neuroblastoma was so vicious.

Gloria cried out to her parents.

*　*　*

Her setback left me and Ring guilty and uneasy.

Are we sure we're doing the right thing? How could we continue? How could we keep people focused on the journey and not make them horrified over watching a child suffer?

"I wonder if people will turn on us, Ring," I said.

Steve had no counter. We shared nervous looks and shook our heads for a few seconds.

I opened my e-mail and found a discouraging message from a man calling the series "sick, self-serving voyeurism." My nightmare was real. My initial reaction was to fire back an overly emotional message about how much I cared for Gloria, but I resisted and instead chose an even-keeled reply. I told the man that, if he actually knew me, he'd see my compassion, and if he knew the family, he'd see how committed they were to spreading a story of hope, even at this dire time.

He didn't write back. Maybe he understood. Or maybe he'd condemned me as some vile journalist who was about to make yellow journalism turn green with envy.

While I believed strongly in the power and purpose of Gloria's story, a fear of failure haunted me daily. If I couldn't do right by Gloria, if I couldn't portray the Strausses with the authenticity and tenderness their tale deserved, then I figured my journalism career would be over soon. The series had become more important to me than food and drink.

I went to my friend, Bishop, for advice. Bishop was no bishop. That was just his last name, but as with Kristen and Dr. Pope, I found entertainment in the fact that Bishop was an integral figure in keeping me sane as I followed a Catholic family.

Sometimes, I called Greg Bishop the Arch Bishop because he's the highest rank of his kind. He was a fellow sportswriter at our paper, but he was being wooed by *The New York Times*, the dreamiest of gigs. I never wrote an important story without having a beer with Bishop and talking it over.

"The next story in this Gloria series is easily going to be the best one," I told him, "and I don't know how I feel about that. Gloria's in bad shape. The family is really being tested. It's the kind of drama we live for as writers, but it just sucks."

"I figured you'd get to this point," Bishop replied.

"I thought I had prepared for it, but actually seeing it is heartbreaking. She can't move, man. It's as close to paralyzed as you can be without being paralyzed."

Bishop fiddled with his cell phone and adjusted his round glasses. A self-described journalism geek, he studied writing styles and reporting techniques, filling his mind with an encyclopedic understanding of the field. He picked up every nuance of storytelling, and it showed in his work, some of the best I'd ever read. He was twenty-six years old and seemed destined to rule the sportswriting world.

"You can't stop telling that story, no matter how hard it gets," he reminded me. "It's too good of a story. People need to hear it. And people are already engaged."

"Oh, I'm definitely in it for the long haul," I said. "Hopefully, readers can handle what's to come. Hopefully, I can handle it."

Bishop posed a question he'd been waiting for the right time to ask.

"Do you think she can get that miracle now?"

"The cynical journalist in me says no way," I told him. "But when I'm not frontin', I have to admit that there's something else going on, something I don't even understand. It's nothing that I can verbalize or even write about, really. You just have to be in that house. It's just a feeling, a belief that something special can still happen despite all the crap she's going through."

"Hey, just imagine if God did heal her," Bishop said. "That would be the greatest newspaper story ever written. You would be on *Oprah*."

We pondered that thought for several minutes, laughing all the while. I imagined Gloria sitting next to Oprah Winfrey, entrancing the audience with her charm and maturity, finding a way to make her dramatic story even more moving.

"If Gloria ever got America's attention, it's over," I said. "It's a wrap. Everyone would fall in love with her."

"So focus on that," Bishop said. "And just write what you know. Whatever happens is out of your control."

"That's very holy advice, Arch Bishop."

"Yeah, I guess. So, you wanna do a shot?"

* * *

In my planner, the terrifying fact was scribbled alongside reminders of birthdays and meetings.

July 10: The last time Gloria walked.

It was July 16. For nearly a week, Gloria had been immobile. Her grandparents flew in from Indiana. So did two of her great-aunts, Bev and Ginni. They prayed and sang and brought an upbeat energy to the Strauss house, but the family's worries increased every day Gloria remained in that bed.

"I can't say I don't fear death," Doug said. "Whenever I fear it, I pray. There are moments that are just gut-wrenching. You don't want to go anywhere. You don't want to see anybody."

Later that night, Doug retreated to his bedroom and wept. He looked at Kristen and fell apart.

"Where's my faith?" he asked. "Where's my trust?"

Not used to seeing her husband so distraught, Kristen reached for the *Magnificat*, a monthly Catholic publication full of spiritual writings. She opened it and happened to flip to a page headlined "What doubt saves us from," written in red letters. She read to her husband, and while listening to his wife's soft voice, Doug stopped crying and went to sleep. Kristen continued to read, however. She turned to the back of the *Magnificat* and looked for the day's scripture, Matthew 9:18-26. She read the words, underlining key phrases.

While Jesus was speaking, an official came forward, knelt before him and said, "My daughter has just died. But come, lay your hand on her, and she will live." Jesus rose and followed him, and so did his disciples.

Kristen underlined the words, "My daughter has just died. But come, lay your hand on her, and she will live." She found comfort in the words, so she continued reading.

A woman suffering hemorrhages for twelve years came up behind him and touched the tassel on his cloak. She said to herself, "If only I can touch his cloak, I shall be cured." Jesus turned around and saw her, and said, "Courage, daughter! Your faith has saved you." And from that hour the woman was cured.

Kristen underlined the quote, "Courage, daughter! Your faith has saved you." She knew this was no coincidence and read some more.

When Jesus arrived at the official's house and saw the flute players and the crowd who were making a commotion, he said, "Go away! The girl is not dead but sleeping." And they ridiculed him. When the crowd was put out, he came and took her by the hand, and the little girl arose. And news of this spread throughout all that land. The Gospel of The Lord.

Kristen underlined the sentence, "The girl is not dead but sleeping."

To Kristen, this was another moment in which God reaffirmed his promise to heal Gloria. She wanted to wake up Doug and share the message. But she let him rest and allowed this sign of hope carry over into the new day.

*   *   *

Doug awoke and prayed harder. Kristen told him about the scripture, and he was re-energized and anxious. Stress was like fuel for him. Worrying made him hyper. Doug talked faster than ever and paced back and forth at an even greater pace. He told more jokes, too. His coping habits were unrivaled.

"I've been able to handle this without losing faith," Doug said. "I think Gloria's whole life has led her to this. But it's just hard. There's a hospital bed in our home. There's a wheelchair in our home. There's medical equipment in our home. We're sponge-bathing her. We're brushing her hair. It's never been this bad."

So he kept praying. Tom Curran came over at night, as he'd been doing for weeks. During this prayer session, Doug challenged God.

"If your will is to take her, please change it," he pleaded.

This was a much bolder request than usual. Normally, the Strausses asked for a miracle but told God they trusted he would do what's best. This time, Doug sat with his eyes closed, hands clasped and head cocked backward, prepared to yell if that's what it took to get a response.

"You're Jesus," he said. "You're God. You can do anything."

Later, I asked Doug why he was so audacious.

"I've always been afraid to pray against the will of God," he said. "Then I thought, 'Why would I come this far and not demand a miracle?'"

"What would you say to people who think you're just hoping against hope and the outcome is inevitable?" I asked.

Every week, I posed that question in some manner. It was a test to see how firmly the family still believed in Gloria's miracle. It was a test for me, too, an opportunity to make sure I was still thinking critically. I could feel my confidence in God rising, but as a reporter, I bleed ink.

"If I had no belief in God, this story would be pretty close-minded," Doug said. "It would be, 'OK, she's going to die. Let's cry our eyes out.' I get hit in the knees, and I get juiced back up by God and Gloria's faith.

"We're not walking blind. We're not defending ourselves from the worst-case scenario. We're turning ourselves to the miracle. We're not masking reality. If we didn't storm the Heavens, I think bad things would happen anyway, so it's not like we're doing any harm here."

Kristen entered the conversation.

"We're not being stupid," she said. "I always worry about what others think, but then I get this stubbornness and I say, 'Who cares?' People ask us all the time about alternative medicine. We did inquire about a couple of different things, but it turned out not to be right for Gloria."

The parents also mentioned that, in addition to nurses, hospice was providing counseling for the parents and their children. Doug and Kristen worried about the escalating emotional toll on all their kids. Gloria was so ill the parents didn't have much time for their other six children. Their friends' parents and other community members would baby-sit them, or they would spend time with their grandparents, or they would hang out with one parent while the other looked after Gloria, but there were few occasions the entire family could be together for long periods anymore.

"We can't act like we know everything that's going on with our kids right now," Doug said. "Kristen and I are going through some things that we don't even realize we're going through, so I know they have issues they need to talk about."

Every night, one of the parents slept on a couch in the den to help Gloria. Doug barely rested on those nights, so I told him to call me if he ever needed to talk.

"Any time of night, man," I told him. "Don't worry about it. If you need to talk, just call."

So, of course, he called at one-thirty in the morning. And he got my voicemail.

"Oh, any time, huh?" he said on the message. "Well, you're oh for one. C'mon, man, you get extra tired driving around in yo Escalade or something? Kristen and I are up, taking care of Gloria, laughing, having a good time. Where's our company? You told me you would sleep with your cell phone and notebook next to the bed. Oh for one! You're oh for one! Haha. Call me back in the morning."

*　*　*

The next story in the series was as good as I told Bishop it would be. How unfortunate. While two editors praised my work, I offered a shy smile and thanked them. On the inside, I was feeling guilty again. Gloria's deterioration was now the fodder for my attaboys.

In the newspaper business, however, there is little time to fixate on a single story. Another day means another deadline, which is great if you've written something horrible, and horrible if you've written something great. For me, the series would continue, so I'd be taking another plunge into something I hadn't done before, something that kept pulling me along, fascinating me despite my fear of messing up.

An upsetting subject needed to be addressed, however. Laura Gordon, a fabulous news planning editor who, along with Bill, the assistant sports editor, helped make my series worthy of Page A1, brought it up. She sobbed with each word.

"What...if...she...dies?" Laura asked. "How...should...we...handle...it?"

I put my head down. So did Bill. Laura apologized for being so emotional, but if Bill and I weren't so needlessly macho, we would've joined her and made one big puddle in the middle of the newsroom. For me, letting the tears flow would've been easier than forcing them back. The three of us sat in silence and sadness for a few seconds.

"It's hard to believe how attached we've come to this girl in such a short time," Bill said softly. "But, yeah, I guess we do need a game plan."

As they devised this plan, I listened and agreed with their thoughts mostly. Then they asked if I should pre-write that last story in case she passed late at night.

"No," I said tersely.

They asked why. I hunched over, put my hands together, raised them to my lips and said it wouldn't feel right to write it ahead of time.

"Right now, I'm so focused on whether she will walk again," I told them. "That's hard enough to deal with, the whole, 'What if she has to spend her last days like this?' But more than that, I don't want to write something from my current emotional and mental state and force it to stand up for who knows how long. I just worry that it would be a stale tribute to her life."

So, they wondered, what if the bad news broke at nine or ten at night?

"One thing about sportswriters is we know how to write on deadline," I said, grinning.

"If you think you can handle it, we trust you," Bill said.

Faith, journalism style.

The newspaper was now in Gloria's position. We couldn't map out an ending. We had to have confidence that something worthwhile was going to happen, and that we would be able to cover it in a special manner. There was no template, no timetable. It was up to the cancer. Or God. We had to sit back, feel our way through this thing and be open to anything. Just like Gloria.

*　*　*

For several days, Gloria had acted like a person who couldn't walk anymore. She was sullen. She was impatient. If she detected pity in the way you looked at her, she shut down. When I visited, I didn't linger near her because I hoped she wouldn't notice my sorrow, but she probably figured it out anyway. Ring spent more time in her space, taking photographs and wondering if he was being too intrusive.

Every so often, he would take a picture and look up at Gloria nervously. She smiled and nodded, letting him know she didn't mind. For Ring, it was affirmation that he belonged here. The man in the white shirt had become a friend, not some paparazzo exploiting an ailing star.

"That meant lot to me, Jerry," Ring said.

Then the photographer of few words opened up a little. He talked about his son, Abie, who was about to turn eighteen. He talked about his daughter, Robin, who was thirteen. He mentioned, as many parents following the series had, that the Strausses' plight made him thankful for his children's health. He also wondered if, in the face of such horror, his family could be so strong.

"I just want to see Gloria's spirits up again," Ring said. "She's normally full of life. I'd give almost anything to see that side of her one more time."

The strain of Gloria's deterioration was affecting everyone. I called Jen to see how she was doing. She talked through tears. It startled me because she was usually the upbeat one, or at least the one best at concealing her grief. We kept the conversation short, Jen was as gracious as ever, and after hanging up, I regretted not saying anything that could relax her. As someone who took pride in being a wordsmith, someone capable of twisting the language in an unexpected manner, I sucked at giving comfort. The disappointing thing about words: It's easier to convey an emotion than to alleviate it.

The next day, Ring got his wish. Gloria perked up and talked more as Alissa painted her toenails. She had been vague with her parents the past week, but now she was telling them exactly how she felt and what she needed from them. Doug and Kristen moved her around so skillfully that they were able to dress Gloria in one of her favorite outfits.

Looking like herself, Gloria told her family she could sit on the couch and watch television with Alissa. Her parents helped her over to the couch, and after an hour, she fell asleep. When she awoke, the pain commenced. She groaned as they carried her back to the bed.

Still, she reveled in her progress. As Kristen read to her, Gloria interrupted.

"Wait, Mom," she said. "Before you continue, I just wanted to say this is how I always imagined it."

Kristen didn't understand.

"What do you mean?" she asked. "Tell me more."

Gloria referred her mother back to their conversation on April 19, the day before Dr. Park called to say she was dying.

"Remember when I told you I feel like it's going to get worse before it gets better?" Gloria asked.

Kristen nodded.

"This is how I imagined it," Gloria said. "I always saw myself in bed, on an IV, and people were all around me and praying. At a time like this, that's when I envisioned getting my miracle."

Near tears, Kristen touched Gloria's face and looked into her eyes.

* * *

I went to Tom Curran to talk about prayer. His ministry, Trinity Formation Resources, helps Catholics understand how to mobilize their faith. To many, religion is a checklist of responsibilities, but Tom specializes in helping people live and share their beliefs.

The Strausses gave Tom significant credit for nurturing their faith and making their prayer sessions dynamic, but he declined to accept the compliment. Just doing his part, he said.

I asked him about the great conflict in praying for Gloria: Is it right to ask for this miracle? He explained the focus was more on the relationship with God than the request.

"You're asking Jesus to come close to this situation and to be who He is," Tom said. "You're saying, 'I want you, Jesus. Come close. Be who you are. And bring salvation.' That's the first miracle. When we say yes to Jesus, and we come and we pray, in some mysterious way, God uses that. I pray with great confidence. I don't come seeking something. I come seeking someone."

It was an esoteric concept. For believers, it made sense. For everyone else, it sounded like a ghost story. I told Tom about my struggles relaying it all to an audience with diverse spiritual beliefs, and he said I handled it well. For the hour that we talked, my neurosis vanished.

"Ultimately, you can only tell it like it is," Tom said. "There's a wonderful theological book called 'Mere Christianity,' written by C.S. Lewis. When I think of the Strausses, I think of them as mere Christians. We tend to think of the word 'mere' as meaning 'only.' C.S. Lewis used the Latin root of the word, which is 'pure.' The Strausses are pure Christians, mere Christians. When you get down to the distilled essence of who they are, that's what you find. That's what you have to portray because it's true."

"That's the easy part of the whole thing," I told Tom. "I've never once sensed any fakeness about them."

"I have been so blessed and amazed by the opportunity to pray for

Gloria," Tom said. "Way more than I've been a blessing to them, they've been a blessing to me. It's just beautiful stuff. It just blows me away. Gloria has been so true to her name. The glory of God has really shone through her in the four years I've been around."

Now that we were comfortable with each other, I talked more frankly.

"So, here's the thing, Tom," I said. "If Gloria doesn't get this healing miracle, a lot of people will think this was all for naught. I almost feel bad leading so many people down this road, even though it's truly what they believe. Is there something I'm missing here, from your perspective?"

"Although it's easy to see it this way, I don't believe the conclusion is, 'Either she's a miracle or she dies,'" Tom replied. "I don't say 'die.' I say she's going to go home. Understand, I know what Jesus is going to do. He's going to show up. His miracle can come in the form of a complete medical healing or a complete, final healing. God will heal Gloria. You're praying in a way that flows with God's healing."

I hadn't thought about death as a victory. It made this journey seem like a two-headed coin. If Gloria lived, *hallelujah!* If she died, *hallelujah!* It sounded like selective belief: Rig your faith to trust that, no matter what, God did right by you.

"That's not easy to write as a journalist, Tom," I said. "I'm not sure I really grasp it myself."

"Let me tell you a story," he replied.

Tom took me back a few months, to March, when his father-in-law fell down the steps of the Curran home. It was a nasty, bloody fall, so bad that Larry DeLorenzo had to be airlifted to a hospital.

The family spent three days praying that Larry would survive. Then Tom felt his spirit shift.

"As we prayed over those days, inside my heart, my prayer began to change," he said. "It was as if God were saying to me, 'Tom, pray that he goes home.'"

Tom called his family and friends together, explained he'd been moved to pray differently, and amazingly, the loved ones changed their focus without much hesitation.

Larry DeLorenzo died shortly thereafter. In the lulls between sadness, the family rejoiced over the end of his suffering.

"I came to be able to pray that the Lord will bring him home," Tom said. "As I've prayed with people through the years, I can sense a shift. You can pray for one thing, but if you're in a relationship with God, He will come close and do what's best. He will answer your prayers. The broken hearts that we have for Kristen and for Doug and for Gloria, in some mysterious way, God uses that. And He will provide a miracle on his own time."

Those words sparked a flashback to my childhood. I could hear the choir singing "He's An On Time God" during service. That unforgettable chorus temporarily drowned out Tom's remarks.

> He may not come when you want Him
> But He'll be there right on time
> I tell ya, He's an on time God
> Yes, he is

"You still there, Jerry?" Tom asked.

"Yes, sorry. So have you sensed a shift at all when praying for Gloria?"

"No, we haven't felt it. It seems like there's more to do. It feels like we can get closer to God."

"So, now what?"

"We pray harder. We strengthen the relationship."

"Is that possible?"

"Always."

* * *

At three in the morning, five-year-old Anthony screamed for attention.

"Dad!" he exclaimed. "Dad!"

Sleeping on the couch closest to Gloria, Doug sprang up and expected the worst. When he opened his eyes, he saw Anthony on the floor.

Anthony was laughing. Gloria was laughing. And now, Dad was laughing, too.

Anthony was showing his sister he could do a one-armed push-up. Doug ran after his video camera, only to remember it was stolen. Then he remembered his cell phone could take a picture.

"Let me get my camera!" he told the kids.

Dad fumbled around in the dark for his phone, smiling, as Anthony's body shook from the strain of holding himself up with a single arm.

"Hurry up, Dad!" he yelled.

Doug found his phone, turned on the camera and started fervently snapping images.

CHAPTER THIRTEEN

OUR SUNSHINE

Doug tried once more to reach me during the sleeping hours. The call went straight to my voicemail again.

"Uh oh, you're oh for two," he said on the recording. "What kind of batting average is that? You'll never be Ichiro if you keep this up. So, it's— lemme see—four o'clock in the morning, and we're up. Anthony just did a one-armed push-up out of nowhere. It was sooooo funny. It almost made me forget that Geezy Deezy has been down for one, two, three, four, five, six, seven, eight, nine days. Today's the ninth day. Can you believe that? Well, I just wanted to let you know that, even though you don't answer your freakin' phone, how much you've meant to us. I didn't know about having a reporter around all the time at first, but it's been great. It's like we're friends, kinda, you know. Well, I consider you a friend, even with your Escalade. Anyway, OK, buddy, talk to you later."

It didn't mean the world to me to hear Doug's message. It meant the whole galaxy. My shoulders felt lighter. No more carrying the stress of trying to earn their respect.

Before I could process Doug's appreciation, Kristen hit me with something even more heartwarming.

"I feel like it's our calling to tell this story," she said that same morning.

If I didn't have a clear sense of mission before, I had one now. I wasn't writing just to tell a good story. I was the conduit for the family to fulfill its purpose. Perhaps the arrogant side of me always saw it this way; the humble side, however, had feared those thoughts were a lot of hooey. Now, all of me was enkindled. My soul burned to write more, to experience more, to make sense of the religious quandaries presented in this tale.

I visited Ring and asked what we should tackle next in the series. He laughed and said we should focus on getting the most recent story into the newspaper. I had almost forgotten about that one. It had been delayed for several days because of breaking news. Despite how much the editors praised the piece, there was always a natural disaster or local controversy or some political issue that could be deemed more important on any day.

Throughout the series, I grew frustrated over the news judgment and said to my friends, "I'm writing about life and death. What's more important than learning how to live and figuring out how to deal with the possibility of death?"

Most of my buddies would pacify me by agreeing. But Karen, my new love interest, argued otherwise. A *Times* reporter herself, she reminded me how difficult it was to get on the front page.

"At least you're guaranteed to be out there with this story at some point," she said. "Who cares when it runs? You're very fortunate. Do you know how many reporters in the newsroom would love to get as much space as you do for Gloria?"

"Yeah, I know. But there's only one Gloria. Can't blame me for finding her. Can't keep her off that front page, either."

"Oh, Jerry!"

The series could never be popular enough or garner enough praise to muffle my defiance. The feeling was something I needed to keep me going, even if I had to manufacture it. In the beginning, I fought to get editors to believe in the project, and I kept my dukes up, anticipating there would be another round to keep the series from falling victim to what I called Editor Fatigue Syndrome.

It was disturbingly common for editors to tire of a story, regardless of whether the public remained captivated. They held too many meetings and overanalyzed our product too much and responded too sensitively to criticism. If twenty people were in a room talking about a subject and two of them shared a viewpoint that differed from the rest, one could say that ninety percent of the people agreed. But in newspaper land, that vocal minority could turn a nonissue into a major one.

As journalists, we couldn't let the world be. We always had to change something. We always had to show off our cynicism. I worried about unnecessary scrutiny of Gloria's story. It was typical writer stuff, really, right down to the maniacal distrust.

But this time I could say my uneasiness was about more than paranoia. I had the Strausses' calling on my fingertips. So I had a purpose, too. There was no stopping me. I felt like an express train. Doug was rubbing off on me.

"You can't mess with somebody's calling," I told Karen. "That's bad karma, baby. Baaaaad karma! Mess around with Gloria, and the newspaper might not print one day. Out of nowhere, printing press broke!"

"Oh, Jerry!" Karen replied, laughing.

* * *

It was three in the morning again, and Gloria couldn't sleep. Kristen had couch duty this time, and as Gloria wiggled around in the hospital bed in the den, the noise stirred her mother.

"Honey, are you OK?" Kristen asked.

By the time she focused her eyes, Gloria was sitting up.

"Honey, are you OK?" Mom repeated.

Gloria said yes. Then, as Kristen watched nervously, Gloria stood, lunged for her walker, steadied herself and guided herself to the bathroom.

Mom grinned wide. It was a miracle, no doubt. Gloria wasn't healed, but she had new hope. Cancer hadn't debilitated her legs.

Kristen wanted to shout for her husband. Instead, she chose to keep it quiet for a few hours so that Doug could experience the shock and joy just as she did.

Later that morning, Doug shuffled into the den and saw his daughter sitting on the couch. While he flashed a perplexed look, Gloria rose and walked toward him. Dad's eyes brimmed with tears.

"You're walking!" he yelled.

"Yeah, I am," Gloria said.

They tapped fists. Then Doug came in for a soft hug.

An hour later, the parents continued to celebrate. It was July 20. It had been nine days since Gloria last walked. Of all the comebacks Gloria had accomplished while wrestling with neuroblastoma, this was the most unlikely.

While the rest of the family exhaled, Gloria walked away from the den, her makeshift bedroom, taking slow and easy steps. She needed to breathe fresh air. She opened a side door and wandered onto the deck, out of cancer's bondage and into the sunlight.

*   *   *

Doug sent a text message to deliver the news.

"Gloria walks!!!!!!" he wrote.

I called immediately.

"Are you serious?" I said excitedly. "You've got to give me the details."

"Well, last night, she was in bed asleep, and we were in the den with her, and all of a sudden, this light turned on, and it woke us up. Then we realized there was no source for the light. It was kind of outta nowhere. Then we looked back at Gloria, and she levitated. We started crying on the spot."

"Really?!?!" I asked, speaking several octaves higher than usual.

"Psych!" Doug replied. "I got ya, didn't I?"

I laughed and countered, "Who says 'psych' anymore? That's not hip."

"I'm gonna bring it back," Doug declared.

Then he offered a true replay of what happened.

"Your child is incredible, man," I told him.

"It's a mini-miracle."

"No, this is huge, Doug. I know she still has a long road ahead, but don't underplay this blessing. Do you know how many people probably thought Gloria would never walk again? I feared it myself."

"Never doubt Geezy Deezy."

"I have to go. I have to rewrite the ending to my story."

Suddenly, the delay of that story made exquisite sense. I thought about it all for a moment. I allowed myself to consider whether this was spiritual rather than journalistic.

What if this wasn't about news judgment?

What if God had just created the perfect ending?

I remembered how much concern I shared with Ring over readers turning against us. I remembered how conflicted I felt about realizing that the latest story, the best in the series thus far, was the most heartbreaking. I remembered the "sick, self-serving voyeurism" e-mail.

After all that, the story got held up long enough for optimism to re-enter the equation. When I told Bill Reader that I needed to rewrite the last few paragraphs, he said, "Glad you told me that. It's running tomorrow."

I chuckled. Of course it's running tomorrow. With this amazing timing, how could there not be some annointed string-pulling going on?

The gospel music returned to my head.

He may not come when you want Him

But He'll be there right on time

I moved on from the musing. That was my problem. I never focused long enough to have an absolute understanding of my beliefs. I could blame my profession for this because journalists spend all their time examining the actions and beliefs of others, but that's a cop-out. I just didn't have the self-awareness or the gall to delve so deeply into myself. Instead, I preferred to be passively contemplative.

For the rest of the day, I visualized a sign that hung at St. Philomena, Gloria's school. It read: "Gloria, You Are Our Sunshine." She was exactly that as word of her latest rally spread, radiating joy and relief to all who supported her.

Their most urgent prayers had been answered. With Gloria walking, the door was ajar for them to pray more boldly. If they were truly seeking the relationship with God that Tom Curran had explained, then Gloria's stunning improvement had to be taken as a sign that they were right to keep asking for a healing miracle.

Hard to imagine, but the prayer warriors were capable of being more ardent.

* * *

To the amazement of everyone, Gloria grew steadily more active over the next week. Her pain had turned docile. None of the aches kept her from enjoying life, and for some reason, the medication wasn't leaving her tired all the time.

"I think we finally got her medicine caught up to her cancer," a hospice nurse told Doug one afternoon.

Doug smirked and replied, "No."

They stared at each other for a few seconds before the father persuaded her to consider it a divine act.

"I don't believe it was a magic amount of pain medicine," he said. "You saw how she was. Look at her now. It's so dramatic."

"OK," the nurse acknowledged. "Something has to be happening."

"That's better," Doug said, grinning.

The Strausses planned a party to celebrate Gloria's progress. Naturally, they chose to make it a holy occasion and opted for a Thursday night Mass on the deck of their home. Father Jim Northrop, one of the many priests the Strausses had befriended, delivered the homily. Gloria sat in the front row, gripped her rosary with both hands and looked at Father Northrop with reverence. She wore a jean skirt and a pink shirt underneath a maroon sweater with pink polka dots. She had spent hours getting ready, and her parents even allowed Alissa to put makeup on Gloria. Normally, they would've said she was too young to wear makeup.

The evening turned out to be the inspiring boost the prayer warriors desperately needed. At the end, they gathered around Gloria, about forty or so people, and extended their arms toward the child to pray over her body. Gloria closed her eyes and rested as the pleas for her healing grew more impassioned.

"You have a huge opportunity to heal her, God," Doug said, half-jokingly. "Look at all the people watching. You could really make a splash."

He smiled and declared, "Sometimes, I talk to God like he's my buddy."

The celebration lacked only one element: Kristen's verve. Typical of the Strausses' never-ending string of calamities, Gloria's rejuvenation merely granted Mom the opportunity to get sick.

Kristen had little energy on this night and would spend a couple of days bedridden. She guessed she had strep throat, which would be her fifth bout of strep in the past year. Her husband worried that the MS was trespassing in her immune system again.

"I'm all right," Kristen said. "It's no big deal."

Then she decided it wasn't strep throat. She was just a little run-down from all the sleepless nights caring for Gloria.

"It happens," Kristen shrugged. "I'll be fine."

Doug countered that stress and exhaustion were instigators for her disease.

"We couldn't handle another exacerbation," Doug said. "Not right now. You can't be sick. I can't do it by myself."

"I'll be fine," Kristen repeated.

And then she yielded to fatigue.

With her mother down, Gloria asked for Jen. On that Thursday night, the celebration ended with her lounging in the den and falling asleep in Jen's arms. She would stay that way all night, comfortable and secure, in a place where the cancer surely wouldn't bother her.

*　*　*

A doctor confirmed Kristen had strep throat again. She spent two days in bed, leaving Doug to handle all the caretaking, housekeeping and child-rearing. He enlisted Alissa's help and maintained control the first day, but on the second, he looked at Gloria and got rattled.

He saw a large bump on her head and immediately feared it was a tumor. He rushed to the bedroom to notify Kristen. She wept.

Then he walked back into the den to get a better look at the bump. He noticed a red dot in the middle of it.

It was a spider bite. By day's end, the knot had shrunk.

"It was rough for about five hours," Doug said. "But life still goes on."

He could say the same about the past four years.

A journey that could've ended in death after a few months had lasted this long, and finality still seemed in the distance. That was the sense, at least, a feeling that belied Dr. Park's expert medical opinion. The calendar turned to August, and on her best days, Gloria was suddenly able to jump with Maria on the trampoline, something she had accepted as impossible a few months ago.

Did Gloria have an uncanny will to live? Or was it the prayers? As her rally continued, I made doubt less of a priority and turned to the possibility of God swooping in to rescue Gloria. Even Tom Curran's message that death was a complete, final healing stopped feeling like a trapdoor to me. The conflict of my spiritual roots and journalistic education still rumbled inside me. However, hope had suppressed that unceasing clash.

It was going to work out, somehow. I just knew. I just trusted.

I began to study Catholicism more closely to gain a better understanding of what the Strausses believed. I took a simple first step, learning how to pray the rosary properly. I realized the rosary beads were more than some doodad for the pious. They were a way to keep track of the many Hail Marys said during the prayer. The five groups of ten beads coincided with the five decades the Strausses and their friends recited. To a devout Catholic, my "discovery" was probably as rudimentary as learning the alphabet. What would be my next challenge? Remembering they cross themselves by moving their hand up, down, left and right?

I laughed at myself, but I wanted to understand Catholics in a fundamental, heartfelt manner. The difference in religious ideologies didn't matter. All I knew was, the Strausses could get closer to God than I'd ever experienced, and any insight into how they did it would be worthwhile.

"You're not just following them anymore," Bishop told me. "You're not just inside their heads. You're in their hearts."

"Guess so," I replied.

"You've been Straussed!"

"Straussed? I kinda like that."

I joined Theresa Brennan and Jessica Morley, the two Kennedy students, at a youth prayer service held every week at the Brennan house. It was soul-stirring to learn that teenagers were praying with the same intensity as the adults. I shared a prayer aloud with them, my first such public act in the three-plus months since I'd met Gloria.

Before and after the service, I interviewed Theresa and Jessica and learned more about their connection to the Strausses. Doug was Jessica's sponsor for confirmation into the Catholic Church.

"Their faith increases my faith," she said.

Jessica compared it to the biblical parable of the mustard seed, found in Matthew 13:31-32, which says, *The kingdom of Heaven is like a mustard seed, which a man took and planted in his field. It is the smallest of all your seeds, yet when it grows, it is the largest of garden plants and becomes a tree, so that the birds of the air come and perch in its branches.*

"Other people, they look at us and think we're in denial," Jessica said. "It's not denial. It's just faith."

Theresa shared how much she's grown throughout Gloria's battle. "The first night I met the Strausses, I remember thinking, 'It's really sad that Gloria is supposed to die in the next three months to three years. Wow, that's pathetic.' Then I stopped seeing it like that, and I felt I wanted to be a part of this. From there, my growth happened pretty quickly, and it's continuing."

Both girls took great pleasure in helping as much as they could.

"They've touched thousands of people, and yet they'll call asking for little things, like if we can run to the store to get Kristen a toothbrush," Theresa said. "To know there's something we can do, it's incredible."

During this particular week, one of those little things included helping Gloria be independent for an afternoon. Doug and Kristen decided Gloria was feeling well enough to go to Wal-Mart with Alissa and Theresa.

For the first time in weeks, Gloria was just a girl, not a patient. She primped to go to the store.

Theresa drove the crew, and when they arrived, Gloria admitted she felt pain in her legs. Theresa found an electric cart for her. Gloria fidgeted in embarrassment.

"Gloria, you know what?" Theresa told her. "You have every right to ride in that. And you look so cute. No one is going to think any less of you."

Gloria agreed to use the cart to move around the store. When they were finished, Theresa said she would pull the car to the curb to make life easier for Gloria.

As Theresa drove to the curb, Gloria abandoned the cart slowly and cautiously. Anyone watching could see the medical port in her chest, but she still felt unworthy of special treatment. So she exaggerated her limp while walking to the car.

"Gloria, what are you doing?" Theresa asked, laughing.

With a mischievous grin, Gloria looked up and said, "I don't want it to look like I shouldn't be riding in the cart."

PART III

ROCK-A-SOCKY

One of Grandpa Clem Miller's handmade rosaries. © Chris Rukan

CHAPTER FOURTEEN

THE ELEVENTH OF AUGUST

It happened in a chilling rush. Pain, restlessness, heavy breathing, anxiety—the symptoms besieged Gloria at once. Doug looked at his little girl in the early hours of a Saturday morning, saw her arms tensing and hurried to the bedroom to wake his wife.

"I need you to come out," he said. "She can't sleep. I can't sleep."

It was a befuddling, sudden descent. Twenty hours earlier, Gloria was fine, active, like she had been for nearly three weeks. The parents' concern turned into frantic worry.

Doug and Kristen stared at each other. *What's going on? How could this happen?* They tried all the tricks they'd learned to calm Gloria. They asked her to focus on the mechanics of breathing—in your nose, out your mouth, in your nose, out your mouth, in your...it didn't work. They asked her to focus on the cross, to contemplate Jesus' sacrifice, to use it to find her own courage, to...it didn't work. They asked her to close her eyes and think happy thoughts.

It didn't work.

The commotion prompted the rest of the children to rise from bed. Gloria grew more agitated as a crowd tried to help her.

"Everybody quit talking to her," Doug demanded. "Give her some space."

The parents called a hospice ambulance. When it arrived, Kristen opted to accompany Gloria while Doug reluctantly agreed to drive the other kids in the van.

During the thirty-minute ride to Children's Hospital, Gloria suffered seizures. The mother prayed. "Be bold," she heard a voice tell her. Then she realized the sirens weren't blaring.

Sweet, mellow Kristen turned stern. She scolded the driver and demanded to know why they weren't allowed to speed. The driver made a few calls and received permission to pick up the pace.

"Hurry!" Gloria yelled. "Hurry!"

As they arrived at the hospital, Gloria knew she was in trouble. She looked at Kristen with fear in her eyes and made a desperate plea.

"Mommy, I don't want to die!" she exclaimed.

Then her heart stopped. Kristen dropped to her knees.

"Do you want to revive her?" a medical staffer asked.

Yes! Absolutely! It shocked Mom that it was even a question. Twenty hours earlier, Gloria was fine. Now she lay unconscious on an alleged deathbed.

Once again, the timing proved eerie. It was August 11, known to Catholics as the Feast of St. Philomena.

* * *

When I got out of the shower, I heard the voicemail alert beeping on my phone. It was Theresa. She left an eerily composed message.

"Hi, Jerry, it's Theresa Brennan. I hope you're doing well. I wanted to tell you that Gloria was taken to Children's Hospital this morning. She's in a coma. I don't have all the details, but I thought you needed to know. You can call me back if you want."

I sat and dropped my head. After a few deep breaths, I called Ring.

"I'm going to get to the hospital as quickly as possible," he said.

"I'm right behind you."

Before leaving, I checked my e-mail and saw a message the Brennan family had sent to the masses.

The family is asking that everyone pray, pray harder than ever. We are not giving up. With God, all things are possible. He can heal Gloria. They have always known it will get worse before it gets better and that has happened. Now we are praying that God will take her cross so that she can have her healthy life back. This time is especially difficult for Doug and Kristen. Please pray that God will give them strength and comfort. Please spread the word to people (e-mail, phone, MySpace, word of mouth, however), we need as many people praying as possible.

I called Theresa back. Her mother, Anne, picked up the phone.

"Is she doing OK?" I asked.

"I think so," Anne said. "But it's such a shock. Let me put her on the phone."

Theresa said she would be fine, said her focus was on Gloria, but her voice cracked as she spoke. She'd heard rumors that Gloria was on life support. She couldn't fathom such a rapid descent. I thanked her for giving me the news, told her I was heading to the hospital and vowed to call with an update as soon as I could.

"Be sure to ask if they need anything," Theresa said. "We're all willing to help."

The drive from my apartment to Children's Hospital took about ten minutes. It felt like ten seconds. My mind raced through every possible scenario. My heart beat as if I were running a distance race. With all that concern and fear, I'm not sure how or if I obeyed the traffic signals.

Doug called as I parked. He said they were in the pediatric intensive care unit on the fourth floor. Apprehensive over facing the distraught family, I paced the halls and took in the hospital's charm. It was a warm place.

It didn't feel like a hospital. It looked like a huge playhouse with medical equipment, with beautiful artwork of animals painted on the walls. There was an entrance named Giraffe, another named Whale. There was a Train elevator, along with an Airplane, a Balloon and a Rocket. For certain, people who loved kids built this place. The designers understood a hospital could be playful and serious at the same time.

I ran into Ring while pacing the halls.

"Have you seen them yet?" I asked.

He shook his head no. He'd just arrived, too. We shared our mutual nervousness and tried to put ourselves in the family's hearts.

"It has to be killing Doug and Kristen," Ring said. "I mean, she was just fine two days ago. What happened?"

In the intensive care waiting room, we shared hugs with Doug. The rest of the family had scattered. Kristen and Diane, Doug's mother, were in Gloria's room. The kids were at lunch with some friends and kin.

Doug sat down and provided an update. Gloria was in a medically induced coma. She had a ventilator doing her breathing. An epic fight neared its final round.

"We're desperate," Doug said. "We just want her to open her eyes."

Ring and I listened to him for the next few minutes. He often repeated, "It's hard to believe we're even here right now."

He wept as he said, "I just want to let you guys know that we're still in this with you. We said we'd let you cover it until the end. Well..."

Tears rushed down his face. Ring pointed his camera at Doug, but his own emotions made it too difficult for him to take a picture. He dropped his camera to his side.

We sat there, heads down, contemplating an uncertain future.

"Do you want to see her?" Doug asked.

"There are more important people than us right now," I said.

"Nope. Kristen and my mom are about to leave. Let's go."

Ring and I hesitated.

"Don't be scared," Doug said. "C'mon."

* * *

There was a crucifix on Gloria's chest. When the ventilator forced air into her lungs, her chest rose to create a reverent effect. Gloria's heart was bench-pressing the crucifix.

Up and down it went. Up and down. Up and down. Focusing on the crucifix helped with the shock. It helped distract attention from the tube running into her mouth and the maze of tubes snaking around her. In that bed, connected to all those machines, Gloria looked much younger than eleven. Crazy, I couldn't remember the last time I had looked at her and seen a child.

Kale Dyer, one of Doug's closest friends, joined us in the room. Kale taught math and religion at Kennedy and coached golf. He was about Doug's age and brought an ideal, even-keeled temperament to the gathering. Doug was overwhelmed, Ring and I were shocked, but Kale stood there, gently touching Gloria's arms and singing to her. We prayed together and retreated to the waiting room after about fifteen minutes.

Within an hour, the waiting area was full of the Strauss family and friends. The kids bandied about, restless. Anthony shouted, "Gloria's heart stopped!" Diane grabbed her grandson's arm and told him it was more appropriate to tell people his thoughts in private.

For the rest of the afternoon, Anthony prefaced any of his remarks by tapping an adult on the shoulder and saying, "I came over to have a conversation."

Diane chuckled over the solemn way he heeded her instructions.

The atmosphere was oddly relaxing. Laughter filled the gaps among the worry. Many of the Strausses' supporters met for the first time and expressed their amazement over how large the family's circle had grown.

But inside those hospital walls, the game was different. Faith couldn't roam freely here. The Strausses had to respect the beliefs of the other patients. They also had to deal with doctors and nurses who were programmed to trust only medicine. The differences between the Strausses and the healers surfaced when Dr. Park offered some blunt reality during a meeting with the parents that day.

"Doug and Kristen, I know you're praying for your miracle," she said, "but she's going to die."

The parents scolded the doctor for being so harsh. They implied that, if she had a stronger faith, she wouldn't be so rigid.

Dr. Park fought back tears. The parents did, too. After four years, their relationship had friction, the worst kind. The bond wasn't broken, but their trust had fractured. It would take weeks for the wound to heal.

On the dry-erase board in Gloria's room, the Strausses wrote their purpose: "We're Here To Glorify God Through Gloria." Their conviction couldn't shield them from the dire test results, though. Tumors had spread to Gloria's brain and left lung. The doctors planned to wean her off the drugs that sedated her, but they couldn't guarantee she would be Gloria again. All the signs pointed to imminent death.

Doug and Kristen wished someone would hit the pause button. Didn't the doctors understand that Gloria was fine two days ago? Didn't they know the parents felt so confident in Gloria's progress that they had accepted an invitation to attend the weeklong Camp Side-by-Side? Did they know Gloria had just filmed a video to send to *Extreme Makeover: Home Edition* and had just done another TV interview?

And now, what? Now death? How could her cancer move like the tortoise and the hare?

The Strausses needed a prayer session. They needed it like Gloria needed the ventilator. Hospital rules didn't allow for such a large gathering in the PICU, however. Doug argued with hospital staff. He wanted permission for twenty people to pray in Gloria's room.

An attending doctor told him they could pray only if they chose not to resuscitate Gloria should something happen while friends and family were gathered around her. Doug turned angry.

"You're telling me that, if we want to pray, we have to be willing to let her die?" he asked, accusingly.

It was more complicated and less crude than that. But the PICU was a different animal, had to be. The unit operated with a larger staff, dealt with critically ill patients and relied on tough, split-second decisions. The people working on this floor carried a swagger easily mistaken for arrogance, and they didn't care much about the perception. They expected you to understand their intentions, follow their rules, and when in doubt, get out of their way.

Doug didn't have that kind of subservient personality. As nice as he was, he imposed his will, not the other way around. After Tom Curran convinced him to be less combative, Doug and the attending doctor settled on a compromise. The Strausses could have a ten-minute prayer session.

"And we'll spend the first three minutes praying for you doctors!" Doug exclaimed.

As he pranced toward Gloria's room, the father said, "He gave me ten minutes. I'm taking at least twenty."

After about twenty-five minutes, we ended the prayer session, shared hugs until everyone had been propped up enough to exit this knee weakening day and left Doug and Kristen alone with Gloria. I drove home, and as soon as I got out of the car, the exhaustion hit me. It made me appreciate the Strausses' resilience. They must've felt this way for months.

Before falling asleep, I sat at the computer and wrote an entry for my online journal.

Today was a day the Strausses have always dreaded. It was the most emotional day I've ever had as a reporter. I don't quite know how to handle it. I'm just operating with good intentions and letting the story guide itself.

Gloria is such an amazing little girl. Following the family's story has redefined how I view journalism. Getting to know Gloria these past few months has made me a better writer, better reporter and a better person.

I hope I will have the chance to tell her that.

Later that night, another group came to pray at the hospital. These were the truest of prayer warriors, the ones who had spent many late nights at the Strauss house. About eight of them tried to get into the PICU. Security denied them. The prayer warriors refused to leave and were taken to a room, where they pleaded their case as politely as possible. A little after midnight, they received clearance to pray over Gloria. Tom, a skilled negotiator, used the breakthrough to establish a prayer exemption for the Strauss family. The Strausses would now be allowed to have twenty or so people come to Gloria's room after visiting hours to pray for an hour. They agreed to keep the door shut and keep the volume down. This, and a few other policy bends, would become known as the Strauss Rules.

When the prayer warriors went to work that night, they noticed a change. When they sang, Gloria's blood pressure rose. It fell when they stopped. They rejoiced over the possibility that they were having an impact. They were certain God was listening.

Gloria was still there, deep within herself, listening. The challenge was figuring out how to bring her back.

CHAPTER FIFTEEN

WHITE CENTER

White Center, Doug's old neighborhood, has an awful nickname: Rat City. Most locals think the label originated with a rat problem that plagued the area more than sixty years ago. Others will tell you it goes back that far, to the World War II era, but it actually has to do with the acronym RAT. Seattle was a Restricted Alcohol Territory during that time, but the incorporated White Center didn't have to abide by those rules, so servicemen roamed southwest of the city to drink without fuss.

Whatever the reason, Rat City residents majored in street smarts. Maybe that's why Doug smelled a rat.

He couldn't disguise his animosity. He despised the bedside manner of the PICU staffers. He hated feeling like the doctors were simply waiting to pull the plug on Gloria. He grew suspicious of everything: the way they were medicating her, the heavy doses of pain medication they gave her before the coma, the dismissive looks they gave him while he spoke in his rapid-fire diction.

Doug walked through the hospital humming his new theme music.

Can't nobody break my stride

Can't nobody hold me down

Oh, no!

I've got to keep on movin'

"You've gone from gospel to rap, Douglas?" I said.

"If they wanna fight, I'm ready for a fight," he replied.

I looked at Doug's T-shirt. It said "Rock-A-Socky" on the front and back. To win this fight, to bring Gloria back, he had to channel Grandpa Miller. Doug even had a gesture, a Tiger Woods-like fist pump, that he called the Rock-A-Socky. To end each night, after prayer, he pumped his fist and figured that, somewhere in Heaven, Grandpa Miller was saying, "It'll be OK. It'll be OK. Rock-A-Socky, it'll be OK."

Doug ranted about everything that upset him. He was harder to keep up with than usual.

"How much sleep you get last night?" I asked.

He didn't know. An hour or two, maybe.

"Why don't you sleep?"

"I will, I will. I have some things to take care of first."

We had arrived at a dangerous place. This wasn't a good time for tension. I kept thinking that if Gloria died like this, in the PICU, with Doug wrestling with the medical staff, the family might shatter. There would be regrets galore, bitterness and pain. If Gloria had to go, better it be like Grandma and Grandpa Miller, with loved ones surrounding them, with song and prayer and praise. Instead, the way things were going, this ending would feel as abrupt and jarring as a car crash.

Surely, the Strausses didn't spend four years doing it right, doing it godly, to fall into a rage over some misunderstandings. Then again, they always expected their payoff to be miraculous.

God wouldn't visit right now. No way. The environment was too poisonous.

* * *

When we entered the room for a Monday night prayer session, Doug and Kristen bared their hearts. They explained their desperation. They admitted they weren't ready to send Gloria to Heaven. They revealed that Gloria's liver was full of cancer, and her kidneys weren't functioning properly, therefore all the drugs that put her in this deep sleep weren't passing through her body well enough to allow her to wake.

"We're not denying that Heaven could be possible," Doug said. "But we have not yet felt like God is saying, 'I want to take her to Heaven.'"

Gloria had been in the hospital since Saturday. Her condition hadn't improved. Nevertheless, her parents found hope again. Kristen heard another voice early Monday morning. She believed it was God talking as Gloria would.

"Let me be free to fall into God's hands," Mom recalled. "And then let Him do His thang."

In Gloria speak, it wouldn't mean to stop hoping for a miracle. Her message would be simple: Chill.

So we chilled.

The basketball coach in Doug shined through as he quoted Shaquille O'Neal, one of the greatest centers ever to play the game.

"Don't fake the funk on a nasty dunk," Doug said. "Don't fake the prayers."

As usual, Doug was just warming up.

"We are not in denial," he said. "My humor and stuff, that's not suppressing anything. We're being very open. If we have problems, we acknowledge them. And one of them, we worry about Mommy and Daddy arguing. I'm just worried about, 'Mom and Dad might have another child.' How about that one?"

Everyone in the room burst into laughter. The parents' openness spurred the most powerful prayer session I'd ever witnessed. Before we began, Doug looked at Ring and asked the crowd to ignore him.

"Don't worry about the cameraman," he said. "Treat it like what it is—a blessing."

As Tom led the group, he referred to Gloria's situation as the "culminating moment of four years." I replayed everything that had happened in the six months since I won that coin flip. I wanted to cry as I thought about how far they'd come, how far I'd come, since February. Because of this experience, I was actually content to be alive and focused on the proper priorities. I was ready to love again. But my inspiration, my spiritual mentor, was unresponsive now. It had been such a rough, rousing, bizarre, beautiful journey. It was hard to grasp how it would've felt to endure this for four years.

"We now realize there is a thin veil between Heaven and Earth, Lord," Tom prayed. "We ask that you come closer, remove that thin veil. Come closer."

From the moment we closed our eyes, the temperature in the room rose. It went up and up and up for the entire hour. It felt as if we were bathing in the sun, only there was no natural light in the room.

I wrote it off as body heat. About thirty people were present, but Gloria didn't have a roommate, so the crowd wasn't as tightly packed as you'd think. But the warmer it got, the more comfortable it felt.

"I can feel the presence of God!" someone shouted.

I was just happy I wasn't sweating. I wasn't about to declare I knew God's whereabouts. If He was so close, I'd have a lot of answering to do. But just in case He had snuck in and placed some kind of coolant in my body, praise be to Jesus for the antiperspirant.

"You've allowed a story about prayer on the front page of the newspaper, Lord," Doug said. "That's a miracle in itself. We just ask you for one more."

We shared a quick glance. I almost laughed, but I saw Alissa, crying. She rested her head atop Gloria's left shoulder and sobbed for most of the hour. I hadn't seen her rattled before. During the day, she walked around the hospital and helped keep order in the family, encouraging her brothers to behave. She was so unflappable that when Jason Prouty, one of Doug's best friends and an assistant basketball coach, visited one day, he asked, "When did Alissa turn twenty-four?"

She was thirteen on this night, vulnerable as everyone else. Her tears weren't a sign of weakness, however. They laid bare how strong she'd been over the past few days.

We sang appropriate hymns, songs like "Be Not Afraid" and "Open the Eyes of My Heart" and "Breathe." The best, however, was the final number we sang, "Take My Life," a song asking God to mold us to be more acceptable in His sight. Even Ring stopped shooting pictures and sang along. The number began with a rhythmic plea.

> *Holiness, Holiness is what I long for*
> *Holiness is what I need*
> *Holiness, Holiness is what*
> *You want from me*

We went home inspired. We also went home feeling guilty that we'd received more than we'd given Gloria, yet again.

*   *   *

The next day, Doug returned to his griping. He thought the doctors were too arrogant. He wanted them to listen. He wanted them to believe his daughter could survive. His venting lasted so long that Joe, his six-year-old son, tugged at his pants.

"Yes, Joseph," Doug said.

"Dad, you know what you need?" Joe asked.

"What's that?" Dad wondered.

"Ho-lee-ness," Joe sang, remembering the "Take My Heart" melody. "Ho-lee-ness."

Doug laughed and relaxed for a while. But his mind ventured back to a recent conversation he had with a woman from the palliative care team, and he erupted.

"You know what she told us? You know what she told us?" Doug said, his voice rising. "She told us, 'I hear over the weekend people wanted to pray, but they had to be in here. That's an awfully small God if you have to be here.'"

The woman apologized for her lack of tact, but Doug was still irate.

"The arrogance of these people," he said. "The arrogance! We love Children's Hospital. Remember what we call it? Hotel Children's Hospital? I feel like a four-year relationship should've brought us more respect than this."

Only a confrontation could rescue Doug from his anger. He needed to talk to the doctors. He needed to sit with them, make sure they heard his complaints, maybe even offend a few of them, then rebuild from there. In the meantime, he returned to his theme song.

> *Can't nobody break my stride*
> *Can't nobody hold me down*
> *Oh, no!*
> *I've got to keep on movin'*

"You know you're mixing two variations of that song together, right?" I said.

"What?"

"Yeah, the original version goes, 'Ain't nothing gonna break my stride. Nobody's gonna slow me down.' Then Puff Daddy and Mase came out with one that kinda sampled that and went, 'Can't nobody take my pride. Can't nobody hold me down.' You're kind of stuck between two eras, Douglas."

He laughed.

"You know how the Strausses are," Doug said. "We don't know all the words. But we can perform."

It seemed there was one way to keep Doug calm. As long as we kept making jokes about music, we could keep him off that rampage.

* * *

Throughout this trying time, people kept dreaming about Gloria. I'm not an expert on the meaning of dreams; I'm not one to say they're anything more than a mysterious representation of what's on your mind. However, these dreams were inspiring.

Jessica Morley had the first one. The night Gloria entered the hospital, Jessica dreamed she was having a conversation with a man. She told him that she was frustrated. She told him she didn't understand why so many people were giving up on Gloria. After listening for a while, the man left her with these words: "You don't have to be like them. You don't have to settle for an average faith."

Jessica recounted, "When I woke up in the morning, those words were ringing in my head, and it gave me a lot of comfort."

If nothing else, I considered it excellent material for the next story in the series. Then I had a dream.

In it, Gloria came out of her coma. She was in severe pain at first, but then she got out of bed and walked, much like she had in the family den the previous month. After a bunch of nonsensical scenes, the focus returned to Gloria at the end. She was running around inside a building, hand in hand with her mother, while people ran behind her. They were following her, not chasing. My alarm went off before they reached their destination.

I saw Kristen at the hospital later that day and recounted my dream. When I was finished, she smiled and declared, "Doug and I and Maria all had dreams about Gloria last night, too."

"Oh, wow!" I said. "Do I even want to know what Doug dreamed about?"

"He said his was something like, Gloria woke up, and he went around introducing her to everyone in the hospital and telling them that they have to believe," Kristen said.

"Go figure," I said. "What about Maria's?"

Maria was drawing a picture about it as we spoke. In her dream, Gloria rose, regained her health and jumped on the trampoline with her. Maria wrote a note about it and would later ask Alissa to read it aloud before the prayer session began.

Kristen and I glanced at Maria's sketch as Doug summoned his wife back to Gloria's room.

"I'll be right back," she said.

While she was away, I checked my e-mail. I had posted a journal entry about my dream. Apparently, I opened a vault. Lori Rosellini reported that two of her daughters, Lexie and Caitlyn, had dreams. Stephanie Squires, a Seattle University student who used to baby-sit the Strauss children, reported that she imagined she was sitting with Gloria when she opened her eyes, sat up and looked around.

It made sense that such close companions envisioned her healing. We were all wishful thinkers, so desirous of one more rally from the courageous child. Then I received an e-mail from a stranger.

He introduced himself as a Pure Land Buddhist and emphasized that it was possible for those from different religions to believe in God but interpret him differently. In his dream, he saw a healthy, happy Gloria floating in sparkling, clear blue water and waving. Then she climbed out of the water and ran around with her siblings, loud and carefree.

By the time I finished reading, Kristen had returned. I showed her the message and told her about the others.

"And what about your dream?" I asked.

It was the most vivid of all. It began with a great riot. Adults and children were sword-fighting. Kristen sensed they were after money. Amid the ruckus, Gloria awoke and rose.

"Honey, your breathing tube," Kristen said to her daughter.

Gloria yanked the tube out of her mouth.

"Mom, I'm fine," she said.

At that moment, the fighting stopped.

*   *   *

The doctors agreed to meet with Doug and Kristen to discuss the father's complaints. He ripped them for not caring enough about Gloria as a person and for looking at her only as a patient on a deathbed. He ripped them for changing medications without informing him and for turning complacent because her case was so extreme. He ripped them for increasing her pain medicine too rapidly and for failing to recognize Gloria's drug sensitivity, which Doug believed caused her body to panic and shut down.

"Dad, when you realize it's not about you, and it's about Gloria..." one doctor replied, unable to finish his sentence because Doug interrupted by pointing and cursing.

He settled down, but only a little.

"You think I'm some punk kid," he said. "I have seven kids. I'm not some punk kid."

Doug voiced his complaints again. He made some suggestions about the medicine and offered to relax if they'd all communicate better. The doctors, the people he'd written off as arrogant and uncaring, responded in a professional and kindhearted manner.

When the meeting adjourned, an understanding had developed, if not trust. The doctor who infuriated Doug apologized. Doug said sorry, too.

Finally, he could muzzle the White Center in him. There was no rat, just a lot of miscommunication. Doug's attitude changed from angry to caustic. He now saw the doctors as people who could help Gloria, not as ruthless nonbelievers trying to rob his family of hope.

Dad welcomed medicine back into Gloria's room. It wasn't the enemy of religion. Gloria required a little of both if she was going to open her eyes.

Doug left the meeting and sang his theme song again. He could ditch the anger but not the music.

> Ain't nothing gonna break my stride
> Nobody's gonna slow me down
> Oh, no!
> I've got to keep on movin'

"I prefer the old version," Doug told me. "It's better. That's just how I think. I'm old-school."

CHAPTER SIXTEEN

TWEETY BIRD

Of all his tight-lipped quirks, Ring was strangest when it came to one subject: himself. He wasn't really shy. He just underestimated that people cared, and he created a shell of stoicism because of it.

My favorite Ring-ism occurred at the end of each day we spent with the Strausses. When it was time to go, he didn't loiter. He didn't engage in small talk. He always said, "I gotta jam," and by the time I could force a "bye" out of my mouth, he was jamming, out of the driveway and down the street.

At the hospital, however, we found ourselves waiting for hours. Our conversations gained more depth, and it wasn't only when we were talking about Gloria. Sitting in the waiting room, Ring opened up about his personal life.

"I'm really wrestling with something, man," he said.

"What's up?"

"Well, my son has this backpacking trip coming up in a couple of days. I told him I'd take him. But if I go, I'm afraid I'm going to miss out on something here."

"I don't know what to say. I want you here, but that's your son. You don't want to disappoint your kids too often, I'd imagine."

"Yeah, Abie hasn't been too happy with me lately. We haven't spent enough time together."

"How old is he?"

"He just turned eighteen this week."

"Oh, so he's got that whole rebellious, independent thing going, huh?"

"He has some legitimate gripes."

"If you need to do this, I can hold down the fort. It might be good for you to get out of this environment. We've been here several days, and it looks like it's going to be a while longer."

"I've talked to my bosses about having someone ready to replace me for a week, just in case something happens with Gloria. I hope she rallies. It's been so incredible to be a part of this."

"And our connection is getting stronger, man. Did you hear Doug call you a blessing in the prayer session the other night?"

"Yes, that meant so much to me. I finally feel a part of this."

"You're a big part of it, Steve."

"It's like, all this time, we've been dreading this possibly happening, and now it happens, and you'd think it would be tougher for us to do our jobs. But they've made it easier for us."

"I know what you mean. You go through something like this, and the bond is unbreakable. I feel like we're an important element to them."

"If I go, I just hope nothing happens while I'm away."

"Well, except for Gloria opening her eyes."

Ring wasn't the only person struggling with absence from Gloria. Grandma Vicki was saddened to be stuck in Indiana while her husband, Pat, made another emergency trip to Washington to be at Gloria's side.

Vicki couldn't make it because she had undergone knee surgery, and her doctor advised against flying. If she had known Gloria would slip into a coma, she would've delayed the operation. Once again, the suddenness of Gloria's collapse had left someone flailing for perspective.

Kristen helped her mother keep vigil from afar. Kristen put a phone to Gloria's ear, and Vicki sang through tears.

I told Ring that story to comfort him. Sometimes, a bond could extend for thousands of miles.

"Just do me a favor if you call to sing," I said. "Practice first. I don't think you have Vicki's voice."

*   *   *

Doug and Kristen called a family meeting. They needed to make sure their children understood the situation. Mostly, they needed to talk about death.

The longer Gloria stayed in a coma, the more the parents were forced to consider that this might be the end. They still didn't feel like God was telling them to give up, but they had to be prepared. Because communication was a family strength, they had to level with their kids, even though only Alissa, then thirteen, and Maria, nine, were old enough to fully grasp what was happening.

Tom Curran advised the parents to focus on the time they still had with Gloria and express everything they felt about her while she was still living. A couple of times, Doug talked about Gloria in the past tense. Alissa corrected him quickly.

"Dad, don't say *was*," she said. "Say *is*."

Each child shared a private moment with Gloria. Later in the day, Doug and Kristen brought them back into her hospital room to talk some more.

They performed these family meetings in an almost clandestine manner, which made the reporter in me paranoid. I wanted so badly to know what was going on. I feared they were saying their goodbyes.

Ring had gone back to the office, but I called him and asked him to return.

"Something's going on," I said. "I have a bad feeling."

Ring returned. We sat nervously and chatted with the Strausses' friends. Many of those loyal faces had become so familiar. Bob Turner and his wife, Chris, were in the waiting room most every day. Mike Prato, the Kennedy High principal, and his wife, Laura, came to every prayer session. Jeff and Karen Fantozzi brought food in a toy wagon, and their daughter, Amy, walked around the hospital with Alissa. Jen was there, of course, and the Rosellinis were regulars. Two of Doug's friends from way back, Frank Genzale and Calvin Shaw, visited often. So did Paul Trimberger, one of Kristen's two brothers.

Every day brought new additions to the cast, too. Gloria had been in the hospital for six days, and I'd seen about two hundred different faces. Two days ago, a couple of football players from the Seattle Seahawks—quarterback Matt Hasselbeck and defensive tackle Craig Terrill—stopped by. Terrill's wife, Rachel, joined them.

I had swapped e-mails with Rachel all week and learned their connection with Gloria. The Terrills met her in February in Wisconsin. Gloria attended former Seahawk Grant Wistrom's Circle of Friends trip, a four-day event that allowed forty children with cancer to go skiing, tubing and snowmobiling.

While in Wisconsin, Gloria charmed all the adult volunteers, especially Craig and Rachel. Their Seattle connection clinched an immediate bond. At 6-foot-2 and 295 pounds, Craig was a giant, tough defensive tackle, but he also was an aspiring musician, which meshed with Gloria's dreams. Craig and his wife were so taken by this energetic, sassy, charismatic child. They said to each other, "That girl is terminally ill?" She was the most vibrant person they had met in some time.

At first, it was strange seeing two athletes in this setting. One of the great things about following Gloria was that it meant I didn't have to face my ever-growing boredom with sports. But this interaction turned out to be a good thing. They saw me as a person, and I saw them as people, and we united in concern for a comatose patient. The experience gave us a mutual understanding that persists today.

I continued to e-mail with Rachel after their visit. During those days in the hospital, I wrote every spare second, just to stay calm. I wrote e-mails. I posted frequently in my Web journal. I scribbled down details in a notebook. Anything to stay busy. Anything to convey how I felt.

When the Strausses called their kids back to Gloria's room yet again, three-year-old Sam asked for a favor. He was playing a video game in a special play area and wanted me to keep the other kids away from it. I agreed. He hit pause and ran into Gloria's room.

While he was in there, Maria came out and wanted to play the game.

"I've got that saved for Sam," I told her.

"So?" Maria said. "He's busy."

"You're going to get me in trouble," I said, laughing.

"No, you won't," Maria assured. "It's me. It's in the family. It's not like some other kid is playing."

Five minutes later, Sam sprinted back to the play area and saw Maria hogging his game. He looked at me and gasped. Then his face scrunched with anger. He balled his right fist, reared back and punched me in the shoulder.

"Sammy, stop that!" Grandma Diane yelled.

I laughed. Only a Strauss kid could transition from the seriousness of a tender bedside moment to the triviality of a tantrum so easily.

*   *   *

Ring chose to go backpacking with his son. He apologized to Doug for leaving at such a critical time.

"If I've learned anything from all of this, it's that your children are the most important thing in your life," Doug said. "I would never come down on you for wanting to be with your kids."

Ring was happy to hear the encouragement, but he remained torn.

"I just don't want it to feel like I'm abandoning them," he told me.

"It's just a few days," I said. "I'll hold it down, keep everything in order. When you get back, hopefully there will be some good news."

"I know," Ring said. "It's just hard."

"Trust me," I replied. "Everything's gonna be just fine."

I shouldn't have said that. Right about then, a hospital media-relations manager kicked me out of Children's. For the past week, Ring and I hadn't gone through the proper channels to be allowed in the building as media members. Doug and Kristen welcomed us, so we followed them and didn't bother seeking permission. But it was against hospital policy, and after arguing with the woman for about fifteen minutes, I left because Doug and Kristen started trying to fight on my behalf. They didn't need the distraction.

"They want me here," I told the woman just before I exited. "We've gotten close. It's like I'm an extension of the family. If I were a cousin who happened to write, would you throw me out then?"

"You can't wear both hats," she said. "You're either a reporter or a concerned friend."

She was right. I hated it, but she was right.

By the time I reached my car, I had received several text messages. Doug asked if I was OK. Jen said she heard what happened and asked if she could do anything. Stephanie Squires, who watched the woman escort me out, wrote a directive.

Never stop writing.

The thought never entered my mind. I went to the office and talked to my bosses, and they called some high-level hospital officials to negotiate a solution. They brokered a deal that would allow me supervised visits for a few hours each day. Although I was too emotionally involved to appreciate it at the time, the hospital made a kind gesture. First, there were the Strauss Rules. Now, we had the Strauss Reporter Rules. Despite a few confrontations, Children's had been about as professional and flexible, not to mention fair, as it could be.

But I had been hanging with Doug for too long. I found my own theme song. During my first supervised visit, I shared a few lines with Doug.

Sometimes I feel like
Somebody's watching meeeee!

"I like that," he said, laughing. "But mine's scrappy. Yours is just funny."

I sat next to Diane in the waiting room after Doug walked away.

"So, what's the problem with you staying?" she asked.

I told her that, because I'm a reporter and not a family member, I'm not welcome to roam freely.

"I think they're afraid I might try to perform a surgery," I joked.

"Well, you tell them that you're my son," Diane said. "I'll adopt you."

Her sweet words warmed my soul.

"OK, so if I'm your son, we have to get something straight," I told her.

"What's that?"

"If I'm your son, that makes Doug my ugly brother," I said. "Be sure to tell him that for me."

* * *

The sign said "Believe." It was made of copper and written in cursive. Carl Buehring, a family friend who played his guitar during the prayer sessions, gave it to the Strausses. They used string to drape it over the wall clock in Gloria's room. As the second hand ticked on that clock, it seemed like a test. I recognized the symbolism. How long are we willing to believe?

Gloria had been unconscious for a week. At times, it felt like months. At times, it felt like minutes. If her condition remained the same much longer, hope might turn futile.

That afternoon, right on cue to stem the developing desperation, Gloria clenched her hands. As her parents debated whether it was an inconsequential reflex, she bit the breathing tube in her month. A nurse asked for Gloria to stop. She obliged.

"She's fighting," Kristen said. "I know it."

"She can hear us!" Doug exclaimed.

A few hours later, nurses rolled Gloria over to change her bed, and she grimaced.

"It's coming," Kristen said. "She's coming back to us."

The doctors had reduced all of the medication that put Gloria into a coma, and in theory, once the drugs passed through her system, she would regain consciousness. They thought it would've happened days ago, but Gloria's prolonged slumber made the doctors pessimistic about whether she would ever wake up. And if she did, there was still the issue of managing her pain, which had gotten out of control, and whether her lungs could handle breathing again. Despite her progress, the possibility remained that Gloria would never open her eyes, and perhaps such an anticlimactic death might be better if intense suffering was the alternative.

The family hoped the doctors were wrong.

"We just want to be able to talk to her," Doug said. "We just want to know what she wants. And then we can go from there. If it's time for Heaven, we'll send her off on cloud nine because God is with us. But if she has more life to live, we're not going to shorten it."

The next morning, Doug touched his daughter and said, "Gloria, good morning, baby!"

And Gloria opened her eyes, her big, blue eyes. Tweety Bird was back—briefly. She had the will, but not the energy, to stay awake.

Family members gathered around her, hoping to see what Doug saw. Several hours passed before she did it again. Alissa entered the room, said hello, and Gloria looked at her.

"It was so amazing," Alissa said. "She recognized me. I could tell."

I sent Ring a text with the uplifting update. He replied fifteen minutes later.

"WOW!!!" he wrote.

Gloria became more lucid the next day. She blew Maria a kiss. However, she reserved her most touching reaction for her mother. Kristen had spent nine days anchoring the family through the shock, through her husband's squabble with the doctors and through her own stress. She tried to rouse Gloria by wearing her little girl's lotion—made with sprinkles of glitter—hoping the smell would bring her back. When Kristen's dry eyes couldn't stand contact lenses anymore, she wore glasses with broken frames all day and declined offers to buy her new ones because that would mean leaving Gloria's side for several hours.

For her poise and persistence, Kristen deserved this special moment. Gloria looked at her, and though restricted by a breathing tube, she managed to mouth three words.

"I love you," she said.

Mom cried. Another prayer answered.

CHAPTER SEVENTEEN

BELIEVE

Doug took the "Believe" sign off the clock and danced through the hospital. Gloria's comeback had restored his defiance. In celebration, he couldn't resist needling anyone in the PICU who doubted his daughter.

He plotted the next step: take Gloria off the ventilator. When Gloria lifted her head slightly and did her best to kiss him, he declared the Strausses had their "hospital groove on" and could conquer anything.

He pushed for the doctors to test her breathing. So they turned down the ventilator for twenty minutes to judge how Gloria reacted to breathing on her own. She did so without a problem. The process unnerved the father a little, however. He grew anxious during those twenty minutes of living breath by breath with Gloria.

"They call the process a sprint," Doug said. "I told them, 'How about we just take a walk to the mailbox and back?'"

Gloria needed to be more alert and stronger to sustain breathing on her own. The doctors would keep testing her, and Dad focused on getting her mentally prepared.

Alone with Gloria, he started coaching. The nurses had to restrain Gloria because she grabbed and bit her breathing tube. When they left, Doug untied her hands.

"Relax," he said. "When the nurses come back with a suction tube, close your eyes. And no matter what, do not touch the breathing tube. Got it?"

"I promise," Gloria mouthed.

As soon as Doug sat back, she tugged at the tube. He leaned forward to stop her, but Gloria pointed at him and smiled. Dad laughed.

"You're playing games!" he exclaimed.

Then Doug interrupted the fun with a serious question.

"Do you want to go to Heaven?" he asked.

Gloria shook her head no and looked at him angrily.

To keep her relaxed, Doug recited the Strausses' special prayer, which ends with singing the names of every family member: "God bless Mommy and Daddy. God bless Alissa, Gloria, Maria, Joseph, Anthony, Samuel and Viiiii-ince-ent!"

When he finished, Gloria gazed at her father and offered an answer to his Heaven question.

"I want my miracle," she mouthed. "I want my family."

*   *   *

If Gloria ditched the ventilator, she could move from the PICU to the cancer wing. The family wanted her to be there, in familiar surroundings, where the nurses knew her well. When the Strausses talked about those nurses, their names rolled off the family's tongues as if they were cousins: Brooke, Shauna, Amy, Melissa, Amber.

While Gloria was in her coma, Tiffany, the first nurse who worked with Gloria four years ago, flew in from California to visit and spent a week helping the traumatized parents care for their daughter.

The cancer wing was on the third floor, one below the PICU, but it might as well have been in a different city.

"It's so much more relaxed down there because it can be," Kristen said. "It's just not as stressful, not so many rules. And they know us. If we have to be here any longer, we'd all feel comfortable back on the third floor."

On day thirteen, the Strausses watched the doctors remove Gloria's breathing tube. Before they took her off the ventilator, Gloria was scared, fidgeting over the thought of not being able to breathe on her own, but she relaxed and handled the process without incident.

She complained of a sore, dry throat but nothing else. She could breathe on her own. She was attached to a machine that monitored her heart rhythm, which was used to judge how well she was breathing. The respiratory staff warned the family that Gloria might endure some bouts of labored breathing, but remarkably, she was doing well.

Two days later, she was on the third floor, back to the nurses she adored, back to the place that triggered the "Hotel Children's Hospital" moniker.

I sent Ring another text update. Once again, he wrote back fifteen minutes later.

Ohmygoodness, that's incredible!!! I cant believe it.

Normally, I'm a stickler for spelling and syntax, even on text messages. But I was too excited to bother Ring with my pet peeve.

"It's like God has given us another chance to breathe," Kristen said. "All of us can breathe, not just Gloria. We're all off the ventilator."

Said Doug: "Now that we've got a chance to heal, let's heal."

The parents paid more attention to their other six children. They got a hotel room near the hospital and alternated locations. Sometimes, Doug spent the night with the boys at the hotel while Kristen was with the girls in the hospital. Sometimes, Kristen was with the boys, and Doug was with the girls. Sometimes, one of the parents would get to spend a few hours alone with one of the children.

The Strausses were tired of being displaced. They had to reunite.

Doug found out the lack of attention affected Maria the most. In the hotel one night, she played a Hannah Montana song, "Make Some Noise," for her father. It took one verse for Doug to understand his youngest daughter was lonely.

> It's easy to feel like you're all alone
> To feel like nobody knows
> The great that you are, the good that's inside
> Is trying so hard to break through

"Play that again," Doug said when the song ended.

Maria hit the repeat button on the CD player. As the song played again, Dad held his daughter.

Then they played disc jockey for the next half hour. Maria picked one of her favorite songs, and Doug played one of his. They carried on, and Doug finished by putting Santana's "Maria Maria" in the CD player. Together, they danced, Dad and daughter, until Maria's loneliness subsided.

* * *

I called my family to share the good news. My parents, grandparents and brother were all overjoyed to learn Gloria was out of the coma.

"That little girl sounds very brave," my mother said.

I asked her about miracles, if she thought they were possible, if she had trouble understanding why some people got them and others didn't.

"It's crazy, Mom. The longer she lives, the more comebacks she makes, I wonder, 'What if?' more and more every day. But then I think, 'Why her? Why us?' It's weird, but... I don't know, it's just weird."

"We say it again and again, but it's true: God works in mysterious ways," she said.

But if you never experience those mysterious ways, what's that leave you with? God works in untraceable ways?

"What do you consider a miracle?" I asked my mother.

"It can be a whole lot of things," she replied. "Sometimes, it's just keeping you safe. Like, you hear all the time about a crime or something happening, and then someone realizes they were headed in that direction but got delayed for some reason and missed it. That can be a miracle. That can be God keeping you out of harm's way. Or if you don't have money and God makes a way, that can be a miracle. Random generosity, random kindness. Someone having a change of heart. Families reuniting when it seems like they've been torn apart. A miracle can be as small as you want it to be, I think. It doesn't have to be some big thing that makes your eyes pop out."

My e-mail inbox was crammed by people pondering the same thing. Some were convinced Gloria's miracle was still to come. Some said her ability to unite the community was the miracle. Others believed it was about providing an example of hope, love and persistence.

I went back to the voice Kristen heard.

When I heal her, I will change the lives of many.

We were a few thousand past many. Only the *when* part remained unsettled.

"Do you believe in miracles?" I asked my buddy, Bishop.

"They're possible, I guess," Bishop said. "I mean, we get to write about sports for a living. That's a miracle in itself."

"I've kinda enjoyed my time away from sports," I said.

Before going to sleep that night, I went to Google.com, typed "miracle," hit the search button, and the search engine told me it had 58,900,000 results for the word. *Miracle* might as well have been an article or maybe a ninth part of speech.

I decided to stop worrying about Gloria's miracle. It was coming; no need to analyze it. When it arrived, we'd know.

During my next visit, I got to speak with Gloria again. It had been more than three weeks since we communicated. I walked into her room, said Hello as shyly as when we met back in April and filled her in on all the people who have been following her.

"You've got a whole mountain of support, Gloria," I said. "It's probably increased a hundred times over in the past few weeks. I've got so many cards and letters and e-mails to share with you."

Gloria smiled and simply said, "Wow."

I'd missed her smile. Glow lit up the hospital with that smile.

"We're all amazed to see you make it back," I said. "We were scared there for a minute."

"I'm OK," she replied. "Nothing to be scared about now."

*   *   *

Gloria and Taylor Freyberg were great friends in life and sisters in suffering. Taylor, who was twelve, suffered from juvenile rheumatoid arthritis. They were open with each other about their aches. They shared a similar level of maturity. Their calamities were also eerily in sync.

Soon after Gloria fell into the coma, Taylor was admitted to Children's because she needed leg surgery.

"Her room was exactly above mine," Taylor said, shaking her head at the coincidence.

After her surgery, Gloria was still unconscious, and Taylor convinced her parents to let her visit. She rolled a wheelchair close to Gloria's bed, leaned over and whispered, "I love you, Gloria. You're going to be OK. We're always going to be here for you."

Taylor came to see Gloria again after she awoke.

"You look fantastic," she said. "I love your big, blue eyes."

Gloria squeezed her friend's hand, looked at her said, "You look pretty, too."

Later, Taylor explained the importance of their friendship.

"It makes it easier having someone like Gloria around," Taylor said. "You feel like you're not alone."

It seemed she would be around for a while. Doug and Kristen were talking about the impossible: Gloria leaving the hospital. Two weeks ago, it appeared she would only do so as a corpse.

Doug crossed his fingers that she would improve enough to go home.

"It's a real possibility now," Doug said. "Wouldn't it be amazing to see her get some sunshine? She would be so thrilled. Right now, she still has to sit in that bed. We worry about how she's handling that. Sometimes, it just catches up to you. We don't want her to get depressed."

Her progress didn't stop Doug from talking about Heaven, however. He was determined to alleviate the anger Gloria felt about the possibility of dying. He didn't think it was healthy. If cancer won, he didn't want Gloria to exit the world with bitterness in her heart.

"But how do you explain that to your child, especially when you're telling her to fight, too?" Doug wondered. "It's pretty complicated."

Tom Curran offered some guidance. He shared with Doug some general thoughts that included a catchy phrase: Jesus is the healer and the healing. Gloria couldn't have one without the other, and if the worst-case scenario in her mind was that she'd *have* to go to Heaven, she needed to realize what a blessing that would be.

I asked Kristen for her thoughts. She agreed with her husband, but she was careful not to force it on Gloria. One parent had to play the good cop on this issue.

"She was so mad at Doug the first time he brought it up," she said. "She's never reacted like that."

"So, how do you tell her to expect to be healed, to live on, but also to prepare for life after death?" I asked.

"I think we're all in that place, though," Kristen said. "Maybe we're not all down to weeks to live, like Gloria supposedly is, but we all have a limited time to live. That's why I don't like it when people say someone is dying of cancer. Why can't they just say they're living with cancer? Why put death at the forefront?"

"That makes sense," I replied.

"I don't fear death," Kristen said. "On the other side, it's life everlasting. Oh, it's beautiful! Oh, we can't even imagine. If that's God's will, I know God will prepare us. But we have to remember nothing is impossible with God. So I don't think you have to pick one or the other. He will show you where you need to go."

I admired the clarity of Kristen's faith. Most of the time, she knew exactly what she believed and refused to budge. She navigated the gray area of religion by sticking to her principles. She was the most steadfast Christian I'd met.

But I doubted the parents would ever convince Gloria that Heaven was the place to be. In most cases, her youth enabled her to epitomize childlike faith. She was just following her parents' example.

This time, however, the choice seemed individual. It was her body, her spirit and her desires. Despite her illness, she loved her life. What could be better than friends and family?

While Doug developed a strategy to bring his daughter some peace, Gloria watched her brother, Joe, curl up next to her in bed.

"I love you," Joe said. "You're pretty."

She was already in Heaven—on Earth.

* * *

Jen invited me to a birthday party at the end of August. She and her husband, Tom, were throwing a big bash for their children, Peter and Mary, and they were including Joe because the three kids had birthdays bunched together. Peter was turning eight, Joe seven and Mary four. I was excited to attend the extravaganza.

The party was at the McCann house. Karen came with me, and on the drive out to Kent, we stopped at a toy store to pick out gifts. When we arrived, we walked into a house overtaken by joyful kids. They were everywhere: in the pool, in the house, in the driveway. So much laughter filled the air that I wished I could grab it from the sky, put it in a bag and save it for later.

The festivities included a popcorn machine, the kind you see at the movies, and a station where the kids made snow cones. Joe jumped into the water repeatedly, trying to splash water on those sitting close to the pool. When he got tired of doing that, he ran through the backyard, hugging all the adults to get them wet.

It was the perfect antidote for stress, except when we took in the scene and envisioned the fun Gloria would've been having.

"She's the life of a party," Jen said. "I wish she could be here with us."

"Maybe next year," I said. "Maybe next week. You never know with Gloria."

The adults discussed Gloria's progress, and the hope that she could be released from Children's.

"Oh, I want that so badly for them," said Laura Prato, the wife of the Kennedy High principal, and one of Kristen's good friends. "It's been so hard for them to be confined to the hospital. You know how active the family is. The freedom to do things on their terms would be so wonderful."

It was merely a dream, however.

Although Gloria was breathing on her own, the tumor near her left lung gradually caused complications. Gloria also relished having the nurses and doctors close by, knowing that she barely made it to the hospital alive the last time. Doug and Kristen chose not to push for a release.

"She wants to have that secure feeling," Kristen said when I called her later that day. "We're in no hurry to leave. The doctors are in no hurry for us to leave. We think this is the right thing to do."

"Any idea on a timeline?" I asked.

Kristen hedged. "Maybe next week," she said. "It all depends on what Gloria wants."

"You think that's realistic?" I asked, pressing her a little.

"Who knows?" Kristen asked. "We're day-to-day, like we always are."

Because they were so alike, Kristen always said Gloria was "a girl after my own heart." © Paul Dudley

CHAPTER EIGHTEEN

ELIZABETH ROSE

The start of September signaled the latest quandary. The school year was about to begin.

Doug and Kristen made a difficult decision. He would remain on leave from Kennedy and stay with Gloria all the time. She would return to their Federal Way home with the kids, attempt normalcy during the day, visit the hospital after school and scramble to return home at a decent hour every night.

It was an impossible challenge for Kristen. She didn't want to leave an ill child behind and didn't want to make her kids fall behind in school. At the apex of her stress, she abandoned her usual sunny disposition.

"I want it to be over, but what does that mean?" she confessed. "If it means Gloria not being here with us, I don't want it to be over."

She shrugged and added, "Sometimes, life sucks."

On the other hand, Gloria's spirits were improving. Her legs were weak and swollen, her breathing was getting slower, but she was happy.

Ring noticed it a few days earlier when he returned from backpacking, and she hit him with a series of questions about his trip. He answered them as thoroughly as he could, flabbergasted that this was the same child who was comatose the last time he saw her.

"I think she's ready to talk about Heaven now," Doug insisted.

"Let's go to lunch and talk it out some more," I said.

"Is *The Seattle Times* paying?"

"Depends on how good of a scoop you give me."

We went to Ram in Seattle's University Village, only a mile from the hospital. Before the waitress came with water, Doug revved up his vocal chords.

"Where we were, in the ICU, that's when you can't lose God," he said. "You can't because Heaven's next. In the ICU, so many people lose God, but that's when you need God the most."

"So...how are you going to approach Gloria about Heaven this time?" I asked.

He pointed to his T-shirt.

"I've got my Rock-A-Socky on," he said. "I've got my cheat sheet from Tom. I've given her a little space. The time is now. I know my Geezy Deezy. We've got our hospital groove on, remember? It's time. She can handle it."

*　*　*

Late that night, Doug leveled with his daughter.

"The cancer has spread to your brain," he admitted.

"Really?" Gloria asked. "Oh, Dad, we've got to pray."

They recited the rosary, along with a nurse. While praying, the fatigued child dozed off several times but woke up and resumed seamlessly. She wasn't even a syllable off the pace. The nurse cried.

The next day, September 4, brought the official start of classes at St. Philomena. Gloria allowed herself a moment to pout, but Dad surprised her with something more important.

Father Tom Vandenberg, the pastor of St. Vincent de Paul Parish in

Federal Way, the man who listened to Gloria's first confession, had come to confirm Gloria into the Catholic Church. Confirmation is a rite that symbolizes the strengthening of a Catholic's faith. Children are baptized as babies, but they are confirmed after they are able to fully appreciate their Christian commitment. Most kids don't receive the sacrament until their teens. Because of Gloria's illness and the maturity of her faith, Father Tom was comfortable proceeding with an early confirmation.

"Now you get to choose a confirmation name," Kristen told her daughter.

Gloria was thrilled. After much thought, she settled on Elizabeth Rose.

"Gloria Marie Elizabeth Rose Strauss—that sounds beautiful!" Kristen exclaimed.

Doug seized the excitement of the moment and continued that Heaven discussion.

"I'm scared of Heaven, too," he admitted. "If God gave me a choice, to go to Heaven now or to stay with my family and risk messing it up, I'd probably choose to stay."

"You would?" Gloria asked.

"Yes, it's OK to be afraid, but you have to allow God to be in control. Gloria, you are confirmed. I acknowledge your fear. I acknowledge my fear, honey. Do you understand?"

"Yes."

Dad made progress, at last. Now it was time for the most persuasive tactic of all.

Tom Curran introduced Doug and Kristen to Dean Braxton, an assistant pastor at By His Word Church in Tacoma. Dean could speak to Gloria in an authoritative manner. He'd been to Heaven and back.

He revisited the memory with brilliant description. It was as if he were still gazing at the sublime scenery. He told Gloria he entered St. Francis Hospital to have a kidney stone treated, and when the doctors blasted the stone, it caused a major infection throughout his body. The infection attacked his vital organs. His heart stopped. His lungs quit pumping. His entire body shut down for an hour and forty-five minutes.

Then, in death's lobby, Dean drifted to Heaven. He knew it wasn't a dream. Dreams come from the mind. This came from the spirit. He saw shiny beings, with limbs and form to their bodies, only they weren't made of bone. They were of a substance Dean hadn't seen before.

"They were so shiny I didn't know who I was looking at, but I came to realize that they could show me how they looked on Earth," Dean said.

More than physical appearances, he noticed their joy. It was on their faces, in their smiles, and they didn't need to talk to communicate.

"Their thoughts were transferred to you," Dean said. "There was no miscommunication in Heaven. No one had anything to hide. We all had pure thoughts."

And the colors, wow, the colors. Dean told Gloria the dullest color in Heaven is brighter than the brightest color on Earth. He saw colors that didn't exist here. The thought mesmerized Gloria.

"Everyone likes to say I came back from the dead," Dean said. "A lot of people joke around and say, 'Dead man walking!' But that's not quite right. I was alive. I was alive with the Father and the Son. Being there is true life. He is not the God of the dead but of the living. Our God is pure life, light and love."

Dean spoke of meeting Jesus. He saw a man with a face like "liquid crystal glass," he said. He described Jesus as being the color of bright, brighter than the sun at noon on a summer day.

"But you can still look at Him," Dean said. "It was like, if you weren't right with Him, His brightness could burn you up. But if you were right with Him, you saw absolute joy."

The first time Dean stood before Him, Jesus said, "No, it is not your time. Go back." The second time, Jesus delivered the message in a firmer manner. Dean cried. Who would want to leave this place? He went back to Jesus for a third time.

"No! It is not your time!" He exclaimed. "Go back!"

Eventually, he did. Hospital transcripts listed him as dead for an hour and forty-five minutes. His wife, Marilyn, also a minister, told Gloria of her distress while Dean seemed lost forever.

Gloria had tons of questions. Dean returned to a general theme.

"Everything is right in Heaven," he repeated.

"Did you miss your family?" Gloria asked.

"No," he said. "You will always want them by your side, but everything in Heaven is just as it should be."

"Can you see your family?"

"Yes, you can. You can see them."

Gloria beamed. She had thought of Heaven as distant.

"When I got there, my grandparents and other family members came to greet me into Heaven," Dean said. "I hadn't seen them in years. They'd been gone for so long. For me, it was very impacting. My grandmother spoke to me and told me to bring back as many family members as I can."

Afterward, the Strausses and the Braxtons prayed together. They thanked God for the opportunity to fellowship. The Strausses thanked God for the Braxtons' message. They all asked for Gloria's healing.

Doug peeked at his daughter during prayer and liked what he saw. She was relaxed, at peace—no frustration, no anger.

"She was a different Gloria," he said. "She was the real Gloria, actually."

*   *   *

My journal had acquired its own personality. I wrote a new entry every two hours, letting my emotions bleed onto the Web, allowing others do the same in a daily "Reader Reactions" post and piecing together updates on Gloria's condition. The journal had grown so popular that, if ever there was a lag between entries, I'd receive e-mails asking, "Where are you?"

The large readership surprised me. Jacqui Banaszynski, the editor who birthed the idea, told me months ago that I could build an online community with the journal, but I thought she meant it as a meeting place for the people who were already following Gloria. But readers from around the world had joined those folks. I received messages from as far away as England, France, Guatemala and Spain. I had the attention of all religions, too. Buddhists, Muslims, Hindus, Jews—they were all among followers who made the journey into more than a Catholic, or Christian, thing. Surprisingly, many nonbelievers stayed interested as well.

"Everybody always says this is a story about faith," one person wrote in an e-mail. "I can't grasp all of that, but I know what the story is to me. It's a story of love."

The online community gave me satisfaction and dulled my fear of failure, but I was proudest of an unintentional service it provided. It kept the entire family informed, and at times, entertained.

From Indiana, Kristen's kin had access to information. From wherever, any family member could track Gloria without inundating Doug and Kristen with phone calls. That wasn't my plan for the journal, yet it became an unexpected gift.

John Miller, the cousin from Indiana, was so compelled from afar that he and his brother, Michael, flew to Seattle. The Miller boys had terrific chemistry with Doug. They were Kristen's cousins, but I could've sworn they shared some Strauss blood. Within hours of their arrival, Gloria commented on the connection.

"Wow, I just love those guys," she told her father. "And they're really good for you, Dad."

During their three-day trip, Gloria further transformed into a spiritual sage. She was on a level that no one had seen before. John and Michael peppered her with questions and listened in awe.

"How about your friends?" they asked at one point. "How are they dealing with this?"

"They're kids, you know," Gloria said. "They like to pray. What I do notice is that, when we have prayer gatherings, they'll come and bring their families. And if we had more prayer gatherings, they would bring their families more, and they would go to church more often."

Michael, a short and thick man with a bald head, reminded Gloria that she had inspired him to run marathons. He started with the Chicago Marathon a few years earlier. He was training for the New York City Marathon that November.

"I'm praying that this will help with all the other prayers and sacrifices to ease your pain, and if it's God's will, to grant you a complete healing," Michael said.

"So, Gloria," Doug said. "You helped John quit smoking, and you made Michael start running. What have you got for Dad?"

She laughed. She glanced into the hallway and saw another little girl trying in vain to walk. Gloria reacted by closing her eyes and offering up her pain to God so that the girl could walk again.

John and Michael shook their heads in amazement. Gloria couldn't walk, either. She hadn't stood in almost a month. Nevertheless, her instinct was to help an ill child she didn't know.

At the end of the Miller boys' profound visit, John shared what he'd learned from Gloria.

He said: "In this culture of death, she teaches us all so much each day about life."

* * *

After Gloria prayed for that girl to walk, I thought about all the sick children at the hospital. I thought about her friend, Taylor. I thought about a woman I'd met in the PICU whose eleven-year-old granddaughter had survived three heart surgeries. I thought about Gloria as a symbol for suffering children everywhere, one extraordinary example of how to power through misfortune that would continue to haunt children regardless of whether she received a miracle.

"We have to do a story about this, Ring," I said.

"How?" he asked.

It would be a weird concept piece, for sure. I didn't know what I was talking about, but I felt there was a story. The feeling would only get stronger.

"Let me get back to you on that," I said.

The Douglas family popped into my mind that night. Over the past few weeks, I'd befriended Jill Douglas and her mother, Stella. They were in the hospital every time I came. And the reason for those frequent visits usually rested on Jill's shoulder—her seventeen-month-old daughter, Alexis Grace.

Alexis had neuroblastoma. She was diagnosed at eleven months, with Jill and her husband wincing at the sight of doctors poking the baby with needles. Just like Gloria, Alexis was a stage-four case, but she was given only a ten percent chance of survival. After twelve cycles of radiation, ten bouts of chemotherapy and an eight-hour operation to remove a tumor, the Douglas family was told that Alexis had three to six months to live. She outlived the prognosis.

"You can't imagine the sense of triumph you feel when your child beats one of those timelines," Jill said. "It's like you're living to defy the calendar."

The Douglases idolized the Strausses. They had attempted to meet Gloria for weeks, but the timing never was appropriate. They did meet Kristen once, however, and engulfed her in affection.

"When I have a down day, I think of you," Jill told Kristen. "I couldn't begin to put myself in your shoes, with Gloria and managing your MS. And I only have two children, and I'm overwhelmed. How do you do it? We love you. We pray for you."

The memory of their encounter spurred an idea: Write a story about Gloria through all the people she's touched. In the process, I could depict the many ways people suffer and the importance of believing in something to get through the despair.

"It's kind of a piece about what we've learned," I told Ring. "We've been at this thing for almost five months and gone through every high and low. Let's tie it all together for people."

"I love it," Ring said. "Let's do it."

We visited the Douglas family a few days later. Jill focused on Gloria's courage, not just in handling the disease, but in her willingness to humanize it. Neuroblastoma is a relatively unknown disease, but it's still the most common source of tumors found in infants, according to Dr. Park. There are six hundred new cases each year. Measured against other types of cancer, the number is small enough for neuroblastoma to be considered rare. For the children it torments, the pain is all too familiar.

"It begins to become a lonely walk," Jill said. "You find that people can't deal with the intensity of the situation, so they go away. It's hard to watch. It's hard to see the pictures, even. We did a slide show once about Alexis' fight and expected everyone to be happy. They were in a state of shock. It is a nasty disease."

"So, is Gloria kind of a partner in this for you, then?" I asked.

"It's her spirit that amazes us," Jill said. "I've met kids like Gloria. Not exactly like Gloria, but the kids I have met like her, they're special and unique. Why? It's almost like these children can reach more people. There's something about them. It's the way she thinks about other people. You don't have to meet her to know that she cares."

We veered off into a conversation about the softhearted nature of children. Jill pointed at her oldest daughter, Austin. One time, when doctors gave Alexis a feeding tube, Austin responded by putting feeding tubes on her dolls. Austin doesn't see her little sister as different. Neuroblastoma is a way of life.

In a grander way, that's what Gloria had done for the Douglas family. She made cancer strangely normal. It was sufferable.

"We make the joke that, if the doctors had told us everything we'd be doing to our child, we would've jumped off a building," Jill said. "I can't believe Gloria handles it so well. She's a face for the disease. She makes people talk about them in a way that they're not just, 'Oh, the kids with cancer.' They're Gloria. They're Alexis.

"I would love to talk to Gloria. Maybe one day, I'll get the chance. I would tell her how much we love her. That kiddo is our hero."

*   *   *

After the interview, Ring and I stopped to see Kristen. The Strauss house was on our way back, and we guessed she could use the company.

She was sitting on the deck, talking on the phone. Vincent rested on her lap. For once, she had time to relax.

"It's the slowest part of my day," she said, smiling. "I don't have to pick up Sam from pre-school for another hour and a half."

"You have new glasses," Ring said.

"About time, right?" she replied.

We let Kristen vent about the difficulty of being away from Gloria. She reflected on everything she was trying to balance. It wasn't simply school and Gloria. Maria had soccer practice. Joe was giving football a try. As an eighth-grader, Alissa's list of extracurricular activities had multiplied. Kristen could barely please any of her children. She had no chance to make them all happy.

"I've had many moments where I've said, 'I can't do this anymore. Please God, help me,'" Mom said. "Then I'm cleaning the house, and I look under some cushions and I see glitter everywhere. It reminded me that God is right here with us."

Kristen told us Doug was just as exhausted. He'd spent one night at home in the past month.

"But in the big picture, we can't complain," she said. "Every day is a miracle."

As soon as she said that, Vincent ran his toy car over her left foot, and the phone rang. Kristen frowned and took the call. I looked at Steve and revised that last line.

"Every day is a miracle," I said. "And a pain."

CHAPTER NINETEEN

PINK AND SPARKLY

Her defining moment came out of nowhere. I guess all defining moments do, really. People don't plan their memories, not their greatest ones, and that's the random charm of them.

No one knew Gloria yearned to say something on the night of September 12. She appeared too tired to be part of this prayer gathering. Her voice was barely audible over the hiss of a blow-by oxygen device positioned just to the right of her face. She asked Kristen to feed her ice chips every few minutes.

With thirteen people gathered around, Doug addressed us with more nerves than usual.

"Tonight, we're not...we ask Jesus not to pass us by every time we pray, right?" he said, turning to Gloria. "So, if you can envision God just holding you in his arms tonight, honey, OK? Sitting in God's lap. And, um, do you mind, uh, telling us something you'd like to pray for tonight?"

Gloria rested her head on a pillow and answered her father, gripping her rosary as tightly as she could.

"I'd like to pray for my body, especially because right now I've never actually...like, never actually thought about what's in my body and what it's doing, how it can spread," Gloria replied, slowly and softly, as if the words were fragile. "And so I really...I really just want to pray tonight for the tumors that are moving through and out my body, whether they're in my head, to my arms, shoulders, stomach, legs and all the way to my toes. So, especially, I just want to pray for my body tonight. But I know I'm not the only one sick...with a sick body. Some of us, and our close friends, are sick, too. Like Taylor. And besides Taylor, many more people we know are feeling badly or might have passed away."

She transitioned directly into prayer with the same slow, straining rhythm.

"So I really just ask right now, dear Jesus, that you hold each and every one of us in mind right now," she said. "Our bodies, hold them tight, and squeeze them hard, right there on their shoulders, so they can feel it."

When she finished, we began to recite the rosary. It was a Wednesday, so the tradition was to pray the Glorious Mysteries. It was the group's favorite day. Family and friends joked they should be called the Gloria's Mysteries because they prayed them so much.

"In the name of the Father and of the Son and of the Holy Spirit. Amen," everyone said to begin, making the sign of the cross.

When it came time for the first Mystery, the Resurrection of Jesus Christ, Gloria led us again. This was her defining moment, an extraordinary supplication against fatigue and labored breathing.

"Dear Jesus, you have risen. You rose from the dead. I ask right now that you raise all of us, not only me, but you raise me up and out of this body in a clear and new way, so I am pure, without any cancer, so that my body is completely...pure...and clear. So I've risen out of this completely...God...but I entirely rise out of it. Not just me, but all of us, that we all rise, rise out in a new, fresh way.

"For any sickness or problems we've had, or for any bad things that we've done, or for any new things we need to do, I just ask that you lift us all out of our bodies, and you give us the strength to get down on our knees."

She moved immediately to an Our Father, but as I peeked around the room, it seemed most people stayed in the moment of that amazing prayer. We didn't know how Gloria managed to say it. We were grateful she did, though.

"She teaches us all how to pray," Tom Curran would say later.

Gloria had lifted the prayer gathering to its maximum intensity. At the end of the rosary, members of the group emptied their hearts for another half hour. They worshipped and cried out to God in earnest, and as several voices competed to be heard, they created a soft humming sound to go with the hissing oxygen device.

"More needs to come," Laura Prato declared, extending her arms into the air. "The work is not done. More needs to come. That's a very strong message I'm getting. Very strong message."

Said Doug: "You hear her praying for all of us. All of us!"

Said Kristen: "We love you, Lord. We glorify you!"

Said Laura: "We thank you, God! More people need to come to you, Lord God."

Said Doug: "Keep guiding us. Every step of the way, Lord. Keep guiding us."

After they finished, they said goodbye to Gloria, one by one, bending way down to hear her because she was too weak to lift her head. Jessica Morley stroked Gloria's hair while they shared their moment.

"I want you to know I'm never giving up on this miracle," Jessica told her. "I love you."

As I took in the scene, I glanced to the right of Jessica and saw a sign hanging on the wall. I hadn't noticed it before. Its message served as a fitting conclusion to an unforgettable prayer session.

It read: "We Won't Stop Praying."

* * *

Ring and I waited out the prayer warriors because we wanted extra time with Gloria. We were working on that story about what the community had learned from her and craved the chance to interview her one more time. We feared she was too drowsy, however.

Jen fed Gloria ravioli while we chatted. I asked Gloria how she learned to pray so well, and she said she just mentions what's in her heart. I told her she prayed in a way I would never be able to, and she encouraged me to keep trying. I asked why she talked earlier about what the cancer was doing to her body, and she recalled a recent meeting with the doctors.

She had noticed a bump under her arm. She demanded to meet with all the doctors treating her. A day later, they came to her room. She quizzed them about it, and they gave several possibilities. Gloria interrupted them.

"Let's cut to the chase," she said. "Is this cancer?"

It could be, they said.

"OK, thank you," she replied. And that was the end of the meeting.

She said she wasn't scared anymore; she just wanted answers. She had accepted everything about her disease.

Jen put down the ravioli and grabbed some pink fingernail polish. She was going to paint Gloria's nails, but the two had a better idea.

"How about we paint your nails?" Jen asked me.

"Can we?" Gloria asked.

I squirmed. Ring egged them on. Diane came into the room and instructed me to muster some courage.

"OK, Mom, if you say so," I said, rolling my eyes.

"You don't have to do it," Gloria said.

"No," I told her. "I will. How about one finger on each hand?"

"No," Jen said. "All ten."

"Really?" I asked. "All right, let's do it."

Ring doubled over in laughter.

"I'm secure in my manhood, Steve," I said.

"Sorry," Gloria said.

Gloria would begin applying the polish to each nail, but she'd doze off during the process, so Jen finished what she started. Whenever Gloria woke up, she'd tell Jen, "Show me." Then she would tell her mother's best friend what needed to be done better. Usually, it meant applying extra layers. By the time we were finished, Gloria and Jen had slapped four coats of polish on my nails.

"Now, we glue on the rhinestones!" Jen said.

"The what?!" I yelped.

"That's how Gloria does hers," Jen said.

I glanced at Gloria, and she nodded in agreement.

"Sorry," Gloria said.

"It's OK," I assured her.

As they finished making my fingernails pink and sparkly, Gloria made a request.

"I only ask one thing," she said. "You have to wear them for at least a day. After that, all bets are off."

"But Gloria, I cover sports," I replied. "What if people make fun of me?"

"If they do, tell them you did it for me," she said. "Tell them you did it for people like me."

For a change, she wanted to be considered a kid with cancer. No question, she was at peace.

I blew on my nails and flapped my hands, trying to make the polish dry quickly. At that moment, Doug and Kristen, who had been away talking to Tom, returned to the room. Doug shook his head.

Gloria grabbed my right hand and placed it in front of her oxygen device. I twitched, uncertain. She held firm and smiled.

"Your nails will dry faster if you use this," she said.

*   *   *

How fitting it was that, a day after hearing Gloria ask God to heal the cancers in our lives, I made a phone call to a recovering alcoholic.

Cliff Wagner had been forced to move from Washington to Falls Church, Virginia, because he boozed himself into unemployment.

For the past two weeks, I had traded e-mails with Cliff about Gloria. He was eager to tell me that she prompted him to put down the bottle. He said he'd been sober since August 27. He rose from a four-day bender on that day, sick and shaking. He visited the *Times'* web site, as he does on occasion, and huffed.

"I was pissed because they kept showing Gloria's picture every day," he said. "But I was hung over, so I finally read it. It was like I was hit by a two-by-four."

"So, what struck you about it?" I asked.

"It was kinda like...let me compose myself for a second," he said, trailing off.

"Take your time," I said.

"I'm fifty-one years old and gruff as hell," he said. "And listen to me." Cliff steadied his emotions and continued.

"You know, it was kinda like the unfairness of it," he said. "I started thinkin', if there's a God, how could He do this? Then it dawned on me that maybe I don't know what it's all about. So I started talkin' to Him a little bit. And one thing led to another."

"So, you just stopped drinking out of the blue or what?" I asked.

"The change was really sudden," he said. "It took me by surprise. I didn't understand that, but it did. I kinda figured, if she can put up with what she's puttin' up with, I can put up with not drinkin'."

I thought the story was too good to be true. Before I voiced my skepticism, however, Cliff opened up some more.

"There's more to it than that," he said. "I've said I'm gonna stop drinkin' before and gone back after two days. To actually sit down and think about a higher power, because of this child, that's what I think changed me. I got this feeling of faith, and that's an unusual thing for me. It's the first time I've let that into my life. This time, I'm approachin' life from a more spiritual angle. I've found it's given me a lot of strength and hope. I haven't been tempted to drink. It's like having God on my shoulder or something."

I was floored by how Gloria had touched him. Cliff faxed me a copy of an essay he'd written for Alcoholics Anonymous. He'd been asked to describe a spiritual experience. His entire piece was about Gloria.

"Every day, I have two meetings," he said. "One is AA. Another is a meeting I have here with myself and God."

During his godly meetings, he lights a candle and reads from what he called the Big Book. Then he talks to God, asking most times for His will to be done.

"I've never been a man of action," he said. "I ask Him to stick his boot up my butt."

"So, let me get this straight," I said. "You just read a bunch of stories about a little girl you've never met and changed on the spot? How does that happen?"

"I drank for ninety-six straight hours," Cliff said. "A lotta rum, a lotta beer, a lotta ice. Then, when I started to come out of it, it was like she found me. When I finished reading about Gloria, I wouldn't stop crying for the longest time. Have you ever cried in your sleep? Neither have I, up until now."

"Wow, Cliff," I said. "Wow."

"I was never interested in quitting," he said. "I just figured I'd drink until I died. I hope God gives Gloria her miracle. He gave me mine."

* * *

Hallie Holton, a friend of Gloria's from Camp Goodtimes, wanted to share a poem. She begged me to print a copy of it and read the words aloud to Gloria the next time I visited the hospital. Hallie was twelve, and like Gloria, she'd mounted a valiant defense against neuroblastoma. I kept my promise and read Hallie's cute, concise tribute to her friend.

> *A generous heart, a warm-the-room personality*
> *A smile that fills every room, a devotion to her family and*
>   *friends like*

No other person I know.
She's Gloria Strauss
And she's my best friend.

Gloria responded with a couple of light claps.

"Wow, tell Hallie I loved it," she said.

It wasn't the only piece of writing I had to share. I showed Gloria a copy of *The Seattle Times* front page on September 16. She dominated the page, looking weary yet dauntless in one of Ring's photographs, her blue eyes gazing at the reader under the headline, "She teaches us all so much each day about life." The story I burned to write had been published, and though the tale wasn't over, it felt like Gloria's message had been sent, the masses had fully comprehended it, and only the conclusion was left.

"Gloria, I couldn't tell you how many people have invested in you," I said. "It's been an amazing, amazing journey."

"When did this run?" she asked.

"Two days ago," I said.

"It looks like good work," she said. "Sorry I can't read it right now." She dozed off.

Before I left, I handed her parents the printout of an e-mail. It was from a convent.

"It's for you," I said. "Someone sent it through me. I don't understand it—I barely skimmed it—but maybe you will."

They read it after I left. It seemed like it was from a nun relaying a message from the Blessed Mother. They weren't sure about the author, but the words rang so true.

I am your Mother of Mercy. I want to refresh you with words, to speak life to you and your angel daughter, Gloria. Your Merciful Savior floods Gloria's soul with Mercy. Divine Mercy is healing your souls.

You are saturated with Divine Grace from the throne of God. My children, I am with you while you wait. In your waiting do not take your eyes off the cross of Jesus, my son, Savior of your souls.

The precious blood of Jesus covers you now.

Suffering may not be understood in the finite mind. It is understood only with faith. It is a language understood with the heart. Your little one is marked with the cross of love upon her forehead. An ocean of Mercy permeates her soul. You, my children, have been given a meritorious cross. Yield to the grace offered to you now. Allow me, your Mother, to work in your hearts and souls.

I am a Mother of Sorrow. My heart burns with pain for my children who must bear a cross with their children, lent to them from the Father's Heart. My Son's Sacred Heart draws you to Himself. Transformation comes to free you of holding too tightly to this world and surrendering all to the Heavenly realm of Grace. You are in this world but not of this world.

The Blessed Trinity dwells within souls who have invited this union of Almighty God's Fatherhood and Sonship. I am crying out to the Blessed Trinity, the indwelling three, to raise Gloria and your hearts to be transformed giving your lives to the Merciful Father.

Jesus, the Prince of Peace, envelops you with His peace. Come, my children, victory shall be won. Surrender your wills to the Omnipotent Gracious God and allow the course of Life to flow accepting this cross and asking that the Grace of acceptance be granted you. Trust that the Father's will is perfect in God's time more shall be revealed.

I ask you to thank God in these moments for the life-giving Grace offered, counting every day as a gift. You are covered with my Motherly mantle and my angels surround you.

"Your hope is in Jesus the Lord. He shall raise you up on the last day. Jesus is with you until the end of time." (Matthew 28:20).

I comfort you, my children. I love you with a Mother's Love through my Immaculate heart. I hold you there, eternally.

Your Mother
Queen of Mercy

Doug and Kristen gave it a thought: Was that a transcription of the real Mary? The woman they pray through during every rosary? Once again, they wondered if they'd been given another sign. Once again, they felt as if they were being guided through this nerve-racking journey. Once again, they sought comfort from a mysterious source.

The next day, Kristen listened closely as Gloria talked in her sleep. It sounded like she was having a conversation.

"The time has come to love and serve the Lord," Gloria said, pausing as one would if waiting for confirmation that the words were spoken correctly.

She said it again: "The time has come to love and serve the Lord."

After another pause, she asked, "Did I say that right?"

"I think she's talking to somebody," Kristen whispered to Doug.

Still sleeping, Gloria flashed a contented smile. Her parents stared with their mouths agape.

Soon after, Gloria became unresponsive. They couldn't wake her. They summoned their family and friends to the hospital, and they asked for their children to be released from school early. An hour later, about thirty people crammed into her hospital room, calmly singing and praying and hugging and crying.

"If this is it, we want it to be this way," Doug said. "It has to be peaceful. No fighting it. Just praising God. That's what we learned from Grandma and Grandpa Miller—how to die. It has to be respectful and beautiful."

And then, nearly ninety minutes after she'd fallen into a deep sleep, Gloria woke up and panicked because everyone was staring at her.

"It's hot," she said. "Too hot."

She asked for ice chips.

Mom ran after the ice. Doug cleared the room.

Brooke James, the nurse on duty, smiled as she hurried over to check Gloria's vitals.

* * *

Jen stayed with Gloria that night. After rushing to the hospital and fearing the end, she couldn't bear to leave Gloria's side. She told Doug and Kristen to take a break and cuddled next to Gloria, laying in silence as the child flickered in and out.

When Gloria zonked out for the night, Jen made a soft-spoken appeal.

"I don't want you to leave us," she said. "I need you and love you too much to see you go. But if you need to, if God is calling you to Heaven, you have to do me a favor. Please be Peter's guardian angel. He needs so much, and you are the one I can trust to look out for him and love him."

* * *

On September 20, Doug turned thirty-three. He kept it quiet, not wanting to upset Gloria in case she forgot. But she knew. Gloria had always been good about remembering birthdays.

She sang to her father early that morning. It wasn't her finest performance, but it may have been her most moving. Straining to breathe once more, she turned a short song into an epic one. She prodded her lungs to cooperate. They did, at their own pace.

Happy…birthday…to you…happy birthday…to…you!

Happy…bir-…thday…dear…Da-…ddy!

Hap-…py…birth-…day…to…y-…you!

"I love you," she whispered upon completion.

"I love you," Dad replied.

"I love…you…so…much," Gloria reiterated.

Doug hugged his child. Gloria fell asleep in the birthday boy's arms.

CHAPTER TWENTY

GLITTER

At four in the morning, Doug looked at Gloria, weaker than ever, and whispered his frank reaction.

"God, I think it might be time to take her," he said, "but I don't know."

He called Kristen, who was sleeping at a nearby hotel. She had stopped shuffling between home and the hospital the past two days. She sensed this moment, too.

Once Kristen arrived, they talked with Gloria, kissed her, prayed and then watched a video of their pilgrimage to Lourdes, France. In 2005, the three took that trip, sponsored by the Knights of Malta, hoping to dip into the storied spring water from the grotto of the Sanctuary of Our Lady of Lourdes. Legend held that the water possessed healing powers.

Near the end of the video, Kristen stood before a large crowd and sang "The Magnificat." She delivered a beautiful a capella rendition in her soothing voice.

My soul proclaims the greatness of the Lord,
My spirit rejoices in God my Savior;
For He has looked with favor on His lowly servant.
From this day all generations will call me blessed:
The Almighty has done great things for me,
And holy is His Name.

Gloria fell asleep amid the comfortable memories. Then the parents relaxed and did the same.

About forty minutes later, a nurse tugged on them.

When they opened their eyes, Gloria was dead.

* * *

Jen called about eight o'clock the morning of September 21. I knew it was bad. She never called before noon.

"I wanted to make sure someone told you," she said, her voice cracking. "Did you hear? Gloria has passed."

"Oh, man," I said, moving to the couch to sit. "Oh, man."

Then Greg Carras, a Strauss family friend, called and wept. After we exchanged fond Gloria memories, I called Ring.

"Steve, it's the moment we've always dreaded," I said. "Gloria died this morning."

We agreed to meet at Children's Hospital within an hour. Steve said he'd handle getting permission from the media relations department.

"Thank you," I said. "I can barely speak."

I went into the closet and searched for the right outfit. It reminded me of Gloria and her love of style. I didn't know what to wear in her honor. I stood there, holding three shirts, and cried.

Doug and Alissa were the first people I saw at the hospital. I hugged both of them. Doug squeezed tighter and tighter. Our embrace must have lasted two minutes.

"We're trying to clean her up right now," Doug said. "We want her to look pretty."

They did it with the help of Keith and Brinn Funai and their two daughters, Emi and Midori. Keith owned a salon, and his family had often visited the past forty days to wash and style Gloria's hair. They would move her body carefully, smiling the whole time, making Gloria feel like the star she truly was.

"When they would wash her hair or the nurses would change her bed or whatever, I would almost always see glitter in the bed," Doug said. "Margarita would've been proud."

No one wanted to let go of Gloria. The Strausses kept her in the room until about three that afternoon. The kids roamed in and out of the room. The boys jumped on bicycles and raced around the third floor of the hospital, a special activity that Children's both allowed and encouraged for patients and their siblings. Little Sam had a crush on one of the nurses, Melissa, so I teased him about it to lighten the mood.

"Where's your girlfriend, Sammy?" I said.

"Girlfriend?" he asked. "I don't have a girlfriend."

"What about your favorite nurse over there?" I asked.

"Oh, Melissa!" he said. "She's my buddy."

Then he pedaled away.

Jen looked after the kids while working feverishly on her laptop. She was Miss Composed, as always. She stayed calm by focusing on one mission: putting together a slide show tribute to Gloria. She edited the nineteen-minute piece as we waited, incorporating videos, photos and songs. I asked if she'd like to take a moment to share some Gloria memories. She declined and kept working.

It was a long, bizarre wait. Ring and I paced the third floor, shuffling from Gloria's room to the nurses' station to the family waiting room.

I looked at the grandparents, Steve and Diane, Pat and Vicki, and struggled to imagine the pain they felt. They outlived a grandchild. Doug and Kristen outliving Gloria was painful enough, but she beat two generations to the casket. Unfair, so unfair.

"Ring, was I crazy for thinking we might've been able to skip this day?" I asked.

"Not at all," he said. "Not at all."

We stopped pacing and settled at the end of a hallway, just outside of the family waiting room. The door was closed because Jen was playing her slide show. We could hear the music as she perfected her tribute. The voice of Shania Twain boomed from the speakers of her computer.

Man! I feel like a woman!

About that the same time, Doug and Kristen looked at Gloria and noticed something different about her. They saw her as a woman. Her body appeared long and full and mature. They kept peering at her, thinking it was a mind trick. But as she lay still, lifeless, with a smile on her face, she was a woman. The parents hoped it was a sign that, in only eleven years, Gloria had enjoyed a full life.

* * *

Ring and I waited patiently for about six hours, hoping to gather more details from Doug and Kristen. Tom Curran arranged for us to meet the parents at their hotel at four o'clock. They arrived on time, holding sub sandwiches, their first meal all day. We talked for more than an hour. It didn't feel like an interview. It was an emotional free-for-all.

"I thought we'd be ready for this moment," Doug said. "And we're just not."

"I just want to make sure I never forget her smell or the sound of her voice," Kristen said.

For the first twenty minutes, we laughed and cried and went off on tangents. Then my inner reporter kicked in. I needed an answer to The Question.

"So, what about your miracle?" I asked.

"She brought Heaven to us," Doug said. "She made Heaven real. Remember when I talked about declaring a breakthrough for our family? Our breakthrough is Heaven."

"I think it's only the beginning of the miracle," Kristen said. "I think there's so much to come."

"But let's be honest," Doug said. "It's bittersweet. We're sad, but we're rejoicing that she's in Heaven. Still, it's just a melting pot of feelings—sad, anger, happy, wondering why."

"She was so much more than our little girl," Kristen said. "She was everyone's. What she's done, I'm so in awe."

"You know what her song is now?" Doug asked. "It goes, *Oh oh, here she comes!*"

We laughed. Only Doug could turn a song called "Maneater" into a heavenly sendoff.

The parents cut pieces of Gloria's hair to keep as relics. They didn't know how they would survive the next few days, but they had to make good on a promise. Gloria wanted to have a huge party when she was healed. She wanted a luau, or something else exotic, something that would be over-the-top and out of character. Now, that party would include a funeral.

"We're sharing Gloria with everybody," Doug said. "That's how we'll celebrate."

Ring and I thanked them for their cooperation throughout the journey.

"I know we're going to stay close," Doug said. "We have to."

"This has been life-altering," Ring said. "You have been an absolute thrill to get to know. There's no way we can abandon that connection. It's been more than just a story for us."

Our goodbye was a prolonged and nervous one on this night. Ring didn't jam. I didn't rush despite a looming deadline. Doug and Kristen didn't worry about all the plans they needed to make. We stood in the doorway, shuffling and swaying.

We were the perfect portrait of our prevailing emotion—confusion. We were four people lost without our spiritual spark plug, wishing time would stop, afraid that tomorrow would be even more difficult than today.

* * *

Hundreds of messages clogged my e-mail inbox the day Gloria died. I didn't bother going through them all. I clicked randomly on different messages. The first two exemplified the never-ending conflict that faith presents.

One of them came from Jessica Morley. She shared a wonderful poem titled "Elevator to Heaven." She began writing it two nights before Gloria died. She captured the emotional response for everyone who experienced that night.

Heads bowed
Eyes closed
We stand as one body united by love
In an elevator to Heaven.

Raise us, lift us
Beyond the understandable
To the perfection of Your will.
Permeate our souls with your grace and
Don't pass us by.

We are here because we believe.
We are here because we see Your face
Reflected in her purity.
You are the Glory of her name,
The breath that brings her life.

Give her a new body,
A healing that extends beyond the
Grasp of the finite mind.
Help us to see you and to understand
In a new and clear way.

We listen as her spirit speaks
Words straight from the Father
The precious veil between Heaven and Earth
Ever so thin.

Tears dance down my face
Unlike any I have ever cried.
Not tears of sadness,
But tears of perfect joy.

The peace is unbelievable.
It flows through my whole being and
Lights up my soul
Burning from within.

A smile rides up my face
Genuine and honest
How could it leave?
After all, I finally understand.
I've discovered the Truth.

Here in this moment
I know what it means to trust,
To let go and to surrender everything
To the one who is in control of the uncontrollable.

The full picture is hidden
And the reality larger than life
But there it stands,
Glittering and shimmering:

A Miracle.

"You nailed it," I told Jessica. "This is beautiful."

On the other hand, there was the second e-mail I opened. The subject line said it all: "Gloria got hosed."

The reader was upset because he'd believed for so long that God would rescue Gloria like in one of those superhero movies. After all that buildup, he figured Gloria only got to outlive her prognosis a little. And most of the time, he said, she was sick and confined to a bed.

"I'm so disappointed!" he wrote. "How are you going to explain this?"

His disappointment brought back memories of a story from the satirical publication *The Onion*. The headline read: "God Answers Prayers of Paralyzed Little Boy." Underneath it, there was a smaller headline: "'No,' Says God."

Now that Gloria was gone, it was easy to consider the journey fruitless. I spoke to Tom Curran about it earlier in the day.

"Yes, it can, from the outside, look like a quick switch or a contradiction," Tom admitted. "People will say, 'I thought you guys were talking about a miracle.' It is not going to make sense to people who are not in the relationship with Christ. It will always appear like a contradiction, like someone is pulling a rabbit out of a hat. But you have to look at it as purely a relational thing. You develop a relationship with Him, and He shows you the way. That's how God's being involved."

It would've been easier if He had held a press conference to explain Himself.

I told the guy who thought Gloria got hosed that the part of the story he hated was also the poignant component. In matters of faith, it always comes back to whether a person chooses to believe. It's a personal decision and a difficult one. It would've been too perfect for God to cure a child with a newspaper standing by to document it. Religion isn't that easy. It can't be.

The guy wrote back: "You make a good point, but I'm still torn."

"In life, we're always making choices," I told him. "We'll see what we want to see. Or not. Faith is a choice. It's not a privilege or a demand."

"Wow, you've learned a lot," he replied.

"Maybe so," I said. "As much as I've learned, I wish I could give you something better, but it's beyond me. I'm not smart enough or spiritual enough, or whatever. I'm sorry, but thanks for caring so much about Glow. She was an original. I'll never forget her."

* * *

Jen went to Disneyland for a few days after Gloria passed. She felt guilty to be away, especially in a place so fun, but her family had scheduled the trip long ago. She would return in time for the funeral, so she tried to take advantage of the getaway to sort through her grief.

How could she go on without Gloria? She remembered all the tough times and the gentle ones, too. She hoped Gloria heard her the night she asked for that one favor.

And then Peter, her autistic son, giggled and said Gloria's name.

It was unlike him. Peter didn't refer to many people by name, and he almost never spoke of someone that he couldn't see. In fact, he only talked about three people—his parents and his cousin, Lindsey—when they weren't around, and he said their names when he had a specific request in mind. Peter hadn't seen Gloria since July, but there he stood, in Disneyland, saying her name and giggling hard, as if he were being tickled.

A smile creased Jen's face. Maybe Gloria did hear her.

"He does not understand how to fake or pretend something like that," Jen said in amazement. "He is too literal. For him to say her name and giggle really meant he saw her, and she either did something very funny or tickled him. There is really no other explanation."

* * *

It was the day after Gloria died. No calendar was necessary for confirmation. The freshness of this grief told time: tears that lingered on faces like rain droplets on leaves, hugs that both comforted and propped, splashes of laughter that temporarily made the sadness recoil.

A small group of family and friends were mulling funeral arrangements at Tom Curran's house. Kristen was lost. She sat on a loveseat, shoulder to shoulder with her husband, and doodled on a yellow notepad. She spent ten minutes letting her pencil absorb the mourning, sketching a sanctuary that resembled a wine glass with pews encircling it. In the middle, she put Gloria's coffin.

The mother tried to position it in the perfect spot, to ensure a beautiful resting place yet respect her daughter's space. Comfort mattered, still. Spend four years staving off death, and no detail seems insignificant.

For a while, this effort quelled the sorrow, but the emptiness within Kristen would swell again, until it was too massive for paper to contain. She started talking to herself. *Is this really happening? Are we really planning this? I miss her so much.*

Rationalizing death proved an elusive, torturous burden for a family that ardently resisted it until the end. The Strausses did not hope for a miracle; they deposited their souls into it. They prayed so hard for so long that God became more buddy than distant deity.

And for what? For grief?

The sadness was obstructing their perspective.

But at the peak of Kristen's pain, she experienced her daughter anew. It seemed as if Gloria's body curled next to her, head in Mom's lap. She heard her little girl's voice. *I'm right here with you, Mom.* Then the once-absent sun slipped through the clouds on the late September afternoon, and sunlight glided into the living room to illuminate her sketch.

Then she saw glitter—mysterious, beautiful, gold glitter. It sparkled atop her notepad and ran across the edges of the coffin in a perfect rectangle. Out of nowhere, glitter traced that coffin, only the coffin.

Kristen tugged at Doug. When he saw the glitter, he understood immediately. They embraced. They knew Gloria lived. No other explanation was acceptable. No other explanation was logical. They just felt it.

Soon, the four others in the room grew curious. Kristen explained, and Tom Curran grabbed the pencil and scratched on the notepad to determine if that was the glitter's source. Maybe one of his daughters had used the pencil previously. No. Maybe there was glitter already on the paper. No. Maybe...no, no, no. This was legitimate, unexplainable. Angelic. This was Gloria.

This was a miracle.

CHAPTER TWENTY-ONE

AFTER GLOW

I dialed Cliff Wagner's number, fingers trembling, certain that I was about to make him start drinking again. Gloria was gone, and I figured his motivation to stay sober would leave, too. I might as well have been a bartender offering free rum.

"Cliff, I'm calling to tell you..."

"I already know," he interrupted.

"So, how are you handling the news?"

"Well, I'm not drunk, if that's what you're askin'."

"That's good. I was worried."

"Don't worry about me. I owe that little girl a lot. I'm gonna try to stay right for her."

And that's how we said goodbye. We guessed we wouldn't speak again. It was best to leave it that way.

Curiosity got the better of me about a year later, and I tried calling Cliff, but his number had changed. Sometimes, the cynic in me sees him passed out at a bar. I hope not, though. I prefer to see a man still learning from Gloria, a man still aspiring to a healthier lifestyle. And even if he isn't, at least she helped him give his liver a reprieve and made him more aware of the cancer in his life.

Gloria died on a Friday, and I spent the most of the weekend making phone calls like the one to Cliff, connecting with many grieving people who followed her story.

I flashed through every emotion that weekend. Anger. Sadness. Guilt, even. Mostly, though, I felt depleted. No more Gloria meant no more telling Gloria's story, which meant no more opportunity to receive spiritual enrichment from her. It was as if, in the past five months, Gloria had become one of my organs, and now I was supposed to function without her.

By Sunday afternoon, I was back to covering sports. My bosses told me to stay home, told me to rest my mind, to rest my heart, but I couldn't. I was too afraid of what else the silence might reveal. The Seahawks played a football game against the Cincinnati Bengals that Sunday, and I drove ten minutes from my apartment to Qwest Field in search of a distraction.

I couldn't escape missing Gloria, however.

As soon as I walked into the press box, my colleagues offered their condolences and appreciation of my work. Tod Leiweke, the Seahawks' chief executive officer, even shook my hand and articulated what Gloria meant to him. While he spoke, I thought of what Kristen had said about her daughter: *She was so much more than our little girl. She was every-one's.* They were probably the truest words ever uttered about Gloria.

The game commenced with trivial delight. Sportswriters traded snarky comments, the crowd upheld its reputation as perhaps the loudest in the National Football League, and the players produced a riveting contest that wasn't decided until the final minute. Normally, it would've seemed like nirvana to me. On this day, it was something to gobble up time.

I was waiting for the funeral, for one final chance to see Gloria. For the first time in my life, I experienced the harrowing delay between a death and a funeral. My uncle Mike was the only person close to me whom I had lost, but I didn't see him in the months before he died. I was a high school student too wrapped up in the concerns of youth to understand how my mother must've felt watching her brother fade over several weeks, only to be forced to revisit the pain a few days later at his services. Mom collapsed into my arms when Mike's casket was lowered into the ground that day. It's the only time I can remember her being vulnerable.

The Seahawks won the game by three points. In the locker room afterward, I shared a moment with Craig Terrill, the defensive tackle who had befriended Gloria.

"How are the Strausses?" he asked, peeling off athletic tape.

"They're just getting by, man," I replied softly.

Craig asked if he could do anything to help. I told him that his wife, Rachel, had mentioned he wrote a song about Gloria.

"Rachel sent me a rough version, and it sounded amazing," I said.

"Actually, give her credit for most of the lyrics," Craig replied. "I just put a little music to it."

"Maybe you can play it for them one day. They'd be touched."

"It would be an honor."

Later, I returned to the press box and wrote a column about the Seahawks' victory, focusing on the up-and-down performance of their star running back, Shaun Alexander. The column felt meaningless. It was just a stew of words and punctuation marks mixed together to satisfy a need. I talked to myself the entire time. *This is it? One day, I was doing the most meaningful work of my life, and now I'm writing about football. Really? Do I even matter? Did I even matter, or was I just fooling myself the past few months?*

I let out a deep sigh. One of my co-workers asked if I was OK.

"Yeah," I said. "Just having a hard time with a transition."

He thought I was talking about writing. I could only wish my transition was as easy as beginning a new sentence.

*   *   *

The Strausses finalized plans for a Thursday morning funeral, with a viewing and rosary scheduled for the night before. They decided to hold the services at Kennedy High, the place where Doug and Kristen met, where Doug was baptized, where students wrote "Gloria, you are our rock" on a boulder the day she died and surrounded it with flowers and teddy bears.

"We thought about having it at a lot of places, but Kennedy just feels right," Doug said. "We don't want a quiet, sad, private funeral. We're sharing her with everybody. The Rock-A-Socky in me says it's celebration time."

"I think you're gonna make it special with that kind of thinking," I said. "It'll be a beautiful service."

"Thursday is also Vincent's birthday," Doug said. "He's turning one. People will probably think we're crazy for holding a funeral on that day, but we're going to make it special. We'll sing to him at the funeral. We'll remind him at every birthday that his sister went to Heaven. That's the place to be. It doesn't have to be a bad thing."

In our last story of the series, Ring and I were determined to produce a fitting tribute to Gloria. So we spent Monday afternoon with the faculty and staff at St. Philomena. About twenty of them sat in the office after school hours and remembered Glow.

To start the conversation, I asked them for words that best described Gloria. Their answers put a spotlight on every aspect of her personality: determination, teacher, honest, fashionista, grace, humble, compassionate, generous, disciple of Christ, finagler, selfless, touching, courageous and fun.

"She taught us so much about the dimensions of love," principal Sandy Smith said. "That abundance of love would flow to whoever was in the room with her."

"And she was really funny," said Nan Merlich, the music and fine arts director. "She liked to tell on her dad a lot. She told me about one time, when the family went up to Canada. They had some of the kids' dirty diapers in the back, and when they got to the border and were asked if they needed to claim anything, Doug said, 'Oh, just the dirty bomb in the back.' She used to say her dad was the rule breaker, and she just followed his lead."

"I know when someone dies you try to make them all out to be some saint, but she really was," said Mary Ruth, who taught sixth grade class and is the mother of Gloria's friend, Aleah.

They recalled Friday, the most difficult day of their professional careers. About fifteen minutes before the children were to arrive at school, the staff learned Gloria had passed. The teachers met the kids outside as they arrived and prepared them for a long day of grieving.

One student, an eighth-grader, broke down, telling the principal, "I forgot to pray for Gloria last night."

Sandy hugged the child and said, "I prayed for her. Don't worry."

Friday Mass turned into an opportunity for the kids to let out their emotions. High school students who were St. Philomena alumni returned that day to seek comfort.

"We didn't know where else to go," they told their former teachers.

"We have a long journey ahead of us," Sandy admitted to Ring and me. "And we also have a great opportunity ahead of us. We're just turning a new corner, reorienting ourselves. Gloria changed our school. She changed the students. She changed all of us."

After two tearful hours, Ring and I thanked the teachers for being so open. They thanked us for telling Gloria's story, but we tossed the praise back at them.

"You played such a big role in shaping who Gloria became," I said. "All we did was put a spotlight on her. We would've been fools not to."

Mary gave us blue ribbons with "Gloria" written across them to wear at the funeral. She also handed me a thank-you card signed by every student in her class. Then Meghan Hoyer, a sixth-grade teacher who would've had Gloria in her class, invited us to her classroom.

"You have to see her desk," she said, motioning for the group to join her.

Meghan had positioned it in the middle of her classroom. Atop the desk sat a framed picture of Gloria, a picture of her classmates, a glass heart, a statuette, a white candle, a cross and two rosaries.

"We hope it moves from classroom to classroom every year," Meghan said. "It's our way of keeping Gloria with us."

"She's with you," Ring assured Meghan and the rest of the staff. "It's just this feeling, ya know what I mean? Hard to describe, but..."

Mary finished his thought.

"There are a lot of kids who've been saying they're hearing little whispers from Gloria," she said. "I've heard that a lot at my home. I really believe them when they say it. It's that feeling that Gloria is still present."

* * *

I stopped by the Strauss house after the St. Philomena visit. Doug and Kristen were so overwhelmed by funeral chores that they barely acknowledged my entrance. I sat next to Alissa at the dining room table and asked how she was doing.

"I'm going through old pictures because we're doing a photo insert for the program, and we have to get them to the printer in a few hours," she said. "Look through these and tell me if you see anything interesting."

When I finished flipping through the pictures, I noticed a piece of paper at the end of the table. It had a blue "American Idol" sticker on it and the words "List of songs for CD" written across the top.

"What's this?" I asked.

"Song titles for when Gloria made her album," Alissa said.

I examined the paper. "CD is called Focused," it read.

Then I looked at the list of the fifteen songs she scribbled down: *cold out side, Its hard to see someones with me, That One Hot summer day, What makes a girl a girl, schools out, I am Over it, Searcerets, Sisters, World Beond, Time flys, alone, The note book, What tears are made of, Shopping, How it happened.*

"There are some pretty deep songs on here," I said.

Alissa laughed.

"That's Gloria," she replied. "You know how much she loved music."

This gave me an idea. The Strausses needed to hear Craig Terrill perform his song live, and they needed to hear it before the funeral.

I went home and e-mailed his wife. Rachel said she'd ask Craig if his schedule allowed it, and a few hours later, we had hatched a plan. Not only would Craig perform, but he would bring Matt Hasselbeck, too, and ask some of his teammates to donate a little money to help the Strausses pay for the funeral.

We scheduled it for Tuesday afternoon. I told Doug I needed the family to gather somewhere for a surprise, and he chose to meet at the Kennedy High chapel.

The Terrills arrived about 2:15 p.m., along with Hasselbeck, his wife, Sarah, and their two-year-old son, Henry. Craig and Rachel shared memories of the winter trip they took with Gloria, reminding the Strausses of her effervescent personality. The family learned a group of Seahawks players had been praying for Gloria for weeks. I realized the line separating celebrity athletes and normal people had been completely erased.

Craig strummed his guitar and sang the elegy that Gloria inspired, "Too Beautiful For This World." It was a short, two-and-a-half minute, heart-rending tune that flowed perfectly with the Strausses' emotions.

> *She let go*
> *She let God*
> *Take her in His healing hands*
> *It hurts today*
> *But it's OK*
> *She was too beautiful for this world*
>
> *Hold me up*
> *Make me strong*
> *With your warm and caring touch*
> *It's her time*

To be held close
Though we miss her all so much
She was too beautiful for this world
For this world

Hold me up
Make me strong
I can't get through this alone
She let go
She let God
Take her in His healing hands
It hurts today
But it's OK
She was too beautiful for this world

When Craig finished, Doug wiped at his eyes and said, "This is just what we needed."

For the next hour, we broke into groups—men, women and children—and it seemed like we'd all been lifelong friends. Matt joked that his little boy, head overgrown with blond hair, had a mullet. Henry responded by pretending to be a scary man, running around the chapel, jumping in front of people and yelling, "Arrrrgh!" If they didn't act frightened, he kept screaming until they did.

"I think Henry, with all his energy, is a perfect match for Sam," I told Doug as the little boys chased each other. "They need to hang out all the time."

Amid the excitement, we almost forgot what tomorrow would bring. In this same chapel, Gloria's body would be in a casket, laid out as beautifully as possible, for a sad community to see her one last time. And I still hadn't come to terms with how I felt about it.

* * *

The next morning, Karen asked if I was ready to handle the sorrow. "I think so," I said, sighing. "I hope so."

She smiled and said I shouldn't be too proud to be emotional.

"It's going to come out at some time," she warned.

"I know," I replied. "I'm open to it. But it hasn't all really sunk in yet. Maybe that's why I haven't had a really good cry yet."

"It's going to come," she said. "And when it does, don't try to stop it."

Karen was the unexpected reward of the perspective Gloria had given me. If I hadn't met Gloria, I wouldn't have been open to a relationship with Karen. My heart would've remained colder than Siberia. But I was in love again, because of Gloria, and Karen proved to be an ideal match. She knew me. She understood me, too, and even though I had been busy with the Strausses, she patiently let our romance develop.

"So, you'll meet me for the rosary tonight, right?" I asked.

"Of course," she said.

Ring and I joined the family for a private viewing later that afternoon. We watched Gloria's grandmothers stand in front of her coffin and weep for several minutes. We witnessed breakdown after breakdown, and then Doug and Kristen suggested we have our moment with Gloria.

"No spectators," Doug reminded us. "Go ahead. Participate."

We shuffled toward the coffin, heads down. We gazed at her in silence for about a minute. I was too nervous to touch her. I had a clumsy streak, and it would be just my luck if I knocked over some flowers, or worse, her coffin.

"Thank you, Gloria," I whispered. "Thank you for all you did for us. It's not going to be the same without you. I'll look out for your family as best I can. Will you look out for mine up there? We love you."

The viewing would last until 9 o'clock the next morning, breaking only for the rosary. About fifteen-hundred people came throughout the night to pray and reminisce and say farewell. Gloria's biggest fans, Jill Douglas and her mother, Stella, were among the visitors. They brought Alexis with them. For me, she was now the face of neuroblastoma.

"I wish we'd gotten a chance to meet her," Jill said. "We've been to a few of these. It's hard to lose another one to this disease."

When we finished talking, it was time to move to the Kennedy gymnasium for the rosary. Before a crowd of nine hundred, Bishop Joseph Tyson set the mood. For those struggling with the idea that a miracle could end in death, he explained a fact about every amazing person mentioned in the Bible.

"They all died!" he exclaimed.

It was a jarring truth. Immortality isn't an earthly concept. Continuing to live means continuing to sin, to defy God, and if we believe in Heaven, we must accept that the real good life is something beyond our comprehension. It's what Gloria realized during her final weeks, and once it became clear, she turned into a spiritual guru.

Bishop Tyson's words helped ease my sadness, and then Tom Curran finished the job. To begin the rosary, he led the first Glorious Mystery, and during his speech before prayer, he abandoned his whisperingly emphatic way of speaking and allowed his raw, passionate words to reverberate through the gymnasium.

"And when we got together, we prayed," he declared, recalling the journey. "No, we poured our hearts out to God. 'God, may this illness not end in death but be for your glory! God, heal Gloria! Bring her wholeness, fullness of life, freedom from this wretched disease!' And we prayed, 'Jesus, come close to Gloria. Don't just drop down a healing from Heaven. Because, Jesus, you're not just the healer. You are the healing. You are her salvation.'

"And he did. In so many powerful ways, Jesus Christ drew near. Many who heard about Gloria's passing last Friday, maybe a few among us tonight, are hurting deeply. Maybe even a bit overwhelmed by grief and left with burning questions. Were our prayers heard? Were they answered? Why didn't Gloria get her miracle?"

I started crying. The tears were uncontrollable, and they came with gasps that made my body shake. I lowered my head into Karen's lap.

"If Gloria had been healed of cancer, she would've been called a survivor," Tom said. "Now, she won't be called a survivor. But she is more than a survivor. She is a conqueror, a victor. You see, cancer never broke her spirit. It wracked her body in pain. It pinned her to a bed. It stopped her heart. Last Friday, it robbed her of breath. But it did not wound her spirit. Instead, it purified it. It transformed it. The more that cancer ravaged her body, the more her soul was displayed in radiant beauty. And many have seen the glory of God shine on her face and be manifested in the way that she embraced her cross."

I couldn't stop crying. Karen whispered that it was OK and urged me not to fight the tears.

"But what about our prayers?" Tom continued. "All those prayers. So many people praying that she be set free from cancer. Gloria did not survive cancer, but she did outlive cancer. And she outlives cancer. She lives cancer-free, forever. Gloria feels no more pain. She's home, safe with God. The healing, the wholeness, the salvation that I prayed for, that we prayed for—those prayers were heard. And not only heard, but answered. And God answered our prayers beyond what eye has seen, what ear has heard, or what has dawned in our hearts. Gloria is held in God's safekeeping."

Karen rubbed my back as I wept, saturating my sleeve. Still hunched over in Karen's lap, I rocked back and forth, talking to myself. *It wasn't in vain. It wasn't in vain!*

"Hear me clearly: Because of the Resurrection, I can boldly say that this sickness did not end in death but is for the glory of God," Tom said. "It is precisely the sickness that has ended in death. Gloria, Gloria—she lives! Thanks be to Jesus Christ, Gloria Marie Elizabeth Rose Strauss lives!"

As Tom closed his remarks, I sat upright, wiped my face and blew my nose. Then I shook my head vigorously. I was a believer. No more conflict.

Those tears were for the clarity Gloria has given me. My faith has been restored. I still don't attend church every Sunday because of my hang-ups and distrust over how people use God to advertise their own agendas, but my relationship with the Lord has become close again. I pray to Him every day. I understand Him better—all because of Gloria.

God didn't ruin my life by allowing a father to believe that I'm too black for his daughter. He helped me find someone better—Karen—and in the ultimate redemption tale, an interracial romance doesn't faze her. She's half Caucasian, half Japanese and all love. Past disappointments vanish quickly when I look at her.

With my heart healed, with my bitterness gone, it was easier to see God through the sadness of losing Gloria. Yet I also realized that I might never trust Him at her level, or at her family's level, but instead of considering it a personal shortcoming, I thought more about the Strausses' extraordinary conviction. I will never believe in anything with the fervor that they believe in God, but then I will never play basketball like Michael Jordan, or think like Plato, or even write like F. Scott Fitzgerald. My limitations illuminate their faith. The Strausses sparkle like glitter, always.

Tom finished with a flurry. He gave Gloria his own heavenly sendoff. I tried to make mental pictures out of his beautiful words.

"If I may be allowed to be dramatic—and that's something Gloria would approve of—last Friday at 6:50 in the morning, Jesus spoke these words of scripture, these words of resurrection, to his beloved Gloria: 'Arise, my beloved. My beautiful one. And come. For see, the winter is past. The rains are over and gone. The flowers appear on the earth. And the song of the dove is heard in our land. The fig tree puts forth its figs. And the vines in bloom give forth its fragrance. Arise, my beloved, my beautiful. And come.'"

* * *

After the rosary, I wondered how the funeral could possibly be more dramatic. That became clear when I saw the procession Thursday morning.

Anthony, the five-year-old, entered riding the shoulders of a family friend and held a large photo of Gloria high, with both hands. Doug and Kristen walked in front of him, unaware of their son's demonstration. Anthony kept a stern look on his face as he lifted the photo with pride.

More than two thousand relatives, friends, students and strangers packed the Kennedy gym to say goodbye. Father Tom Vandenberg gave the homily and recalled listening to Gloria's first confession.

"You're really nice," she told him when she was done. "Like a grandpa."

Father Tom had a simple message: Celebrate Gloria's life. She deserved it.

"This is death with dignity," he said. "This is a celebration of life to the end."

The crowd laughed during the light moments of his sermon. Father Tom hit every note, and true to Gloria's personality, he sang for emphasis.

"How can we keep from singing?" he crooned throughout his remarks.

I chuckled and remembered the many songs that brought joy to a brutal journey. When I met Gloria, she was singing. When she fell into a coma, Doug and I shared theme music. When she died, she left the world hearing her mother performing "The Magnificat."

We had to sing at her funeral.

"We are very broken, but how can we keep from singing?" Doug asked during his eulogy. "How can we keep from singing? She was so beautiful. Her legacy will reign."

In that packed gym, Doug declared victory over cancer, over skepticism, over grief. He pretended to be a choir conductor, waving his arms and commanding us to carol once more. With a couple thousand folks harmonizing, the words boomed through the building, leaving an uplifting impression. We put to rest Gloria's fear that people would lose their faith if she died. We still believed. We believed even stronger now. Hope prevailed in our voices.

How can we keep from singing?

Big sister Alissa said of Gloria: "She was my best friend, and I felt it was my job to be a good example for her. But she was the perfect example for me."
© Paul Dudley

EPILOGUE

My lady loves cherry blossoms. Every spring, Karen hurries over to the Quad at the University of Washington to see the trees in full bloom. She tries to anticipate the exact day they will look their most exquisite, hoping to enjoy optimal basking.

The spring after we started dating, Karen tried to persuade me to go see them. I balked. I asked, "What's the big deal?" She told me they were so pretty—a pinkish white—yet they were so fleeting. In a matter of weeks, they would yield to their transient nature and disappear, unable to be relished again until the next spring.

"You go without me this time, and maybe next year I'll go with you," I told her. "I've got a lot on my plate."

I didn't appreciate those cherry blossom trees until Gloria died. Her eleven years were much like those precious, gorgeous weeks Karen looks forward to each year. Gloria was pretty, yet fleeting. As soon as the public came to adore her, she was gone. What a gift it was to experience her beauty, if only for a short time.

Now, I don't hesitate to accompany Karen to the Quad. It's another way to heal.

In the months since Gloria's death, those who love her have persevered by keeping her close. The pain is unmanageable only during the moments when her presence seems to be fading, when time and tasks lead people away from thinking about her. By staying connected with the Strausses, I've learned that moving on is a misguided notion. Comfort comes not from accepting death but from learning how to keep a loved one alive.

It's why Doug quit teaching and coaching at Kennedy to establish a nonprofit organization to honor his daughter. He teamed with his good friend, Bob Turner, and created Gloria's Angels. Their mission: To do what others did for the Strausses. They aim to provide practical help and build communities of support for families caring for seriously ill relatives. They've helped more than thirty families in their first two years, organizing teams that help with everything from cleaning their homes to providing transportation to assisting with fundraising.

As the family's sole provider, Doug took a huge risk devoting himself full time to Gloria's Angels, but he's managed to make it work financially by supplementing his meager nonprofit salary with a few speaking engagements and some leadership counseling gigs.

"We've always said that if money is our only problem, then we have no problems," Doug says. "Maybe I'm fooling myself, but we're making it. If we start having trouble, there's always the McDonald's drive-through."

Doug and Kristen accept every invitation they get to talk about Gloria. Mostly, they do those for free. They've become coveted speakers, traveling to churches in the region and receiving as much inspiration as they give. At every stop, they've been buoyed by strangers expressing what Gloria means to them.

While in Poulsbo less than a month after Gloria passed, a woman told them that she talks to Gloria often. Once, just before Gloria's funeral, she prayed for Gloria's intercession to help find her neighbor's missing dog.

"Gloria, tug on Jesus' sleeve and help us find this dog, please," she said.

Three days after the woman began praying, the dog returned home, clean and groomed. The woman recorded the date and time of the dog's reemergence—Thursday, September 27, 2007, at 10 a.m.—and realized that was when Gloria's funeral started.

* * *

Ring and I have remained close, and we've both stayed in touch with the family. I talk to Doug five times a week and to Kristen about every other week.

"It's weird," Doug says whenever we go a few days without talking. "We used to talk every day. Some things about the struggle, I don't miss, but some things I do. And our talks are definitely something I miss."

I feel the same about Doug and his family. We've vowed to keep walking with each other. The font of our bond is gone, but the passion to maintain it remains.

Shortly after Gloria died, Doug and Kristen gave Alissa the cell phone she long desired, and she sends me text messages on occasion, which is a double positive. First, if a teenager is volunteering her attention, it means I am unequivocally cool. More important, though, it's heartening to know Alissa sees me as more than the guy with the pen and notepad.

"Hope u dont mind me writing," she typed once.

Of course not.

"Its just that u were around all the time."

Yep, and it was a joy.

"Its hard 2 go back 2 normal. Whats normal anymore?"

Alissa shared a poem she wrote about Gloria titled "I Loved Her So Much." Reading it gave me a greater understanding of her heartache.

> *The phone rang; she answered*
> *The Call ended; the atmosphere changed*
> *Tears began to stream,*
> *As the interruption woke my dream.*
> *I loved her so much.*
>
> *The ride from the hotel was quick.*
> *The ride up the elevator was quick.*

Ugh, her life was too quick.
I stepped out onto the third floor;
My stomach dropped
I loved her so much.

It was quiet and still.
I could barely walk.
Confused, Scared, Sad, Depressed
I am looking at my sister, but she's not really there
I loved her so much.

Crying, Crying, Crying
Mourning, Mourning, Mourning
"I wanted her with me"
"I wanted her with ME"
I loved her so much.

The time was up,
I had to go.
Gloria is with me,
This I will always know.
I loved her so much.

"You have a gift with words, Alissa," I told her. "I thought you were more of a math whiz like your dad."

She giggled. Since then, Alissa has confided in me and asked for advice. She has moved onto high school—Kennedy, of course—and fully embraced her big-sister responsibilities.

Her greatest regret is that she wished she had been around more during Gloria's final days, to say everything she wanted to tell her sister and to have more memories. It's similar to the guilt Kristen feels because, a few days before Gloria died, she asked her mother for a hug, but Kristen was so intent on getting her daughter more ice chips that she temporarily ignored the request. Once Kristen returned with the ice, she walked over to hug Gloria.

"No," Gloria said softly. "The moment has passed."

Kristen punishes herself for caring more about keeping Gloria's mouth moist than giving her the affection she needed. The memory brings her to tears.

"I just wish I had appreciated how precious those moments are," she told me once.

"Don't judge yourself too harshly about that," I replied. "The one thing I know for sure is that Gloria understood, better than anybody, how much her family loved her. I think she was at total peace about that. You know how, even if something turns out wonderful, you never get it perfect? You know how you're always looking at what you could do better? I think that is God's way of keeping us humble. The end of her life was as touching as it could be, but you made a little mistake with the hug, and now you have something that will help make you an even better person."

"I guess you're right," Kristen said. "Thank you for saying that. I like the way you think."

I laughed. She taught me to think that way.

The rest of the family has wrestled with missing Gloria, too. Little Sam Strauss will often say, "I wanna die so I can go see Gloria." He blows kisses to the sky, and whenever he receives a balloon at a restaurant, he lets it go and imagines it flying to heaven.

Doug and Kristen talk regularly to their children about Gloria. They share memories freely. They pray to her. They recall the gut-wrenching moments and turn them into healing opportunities.

"The cancer's not in our home anymore," Kristen says, crying. "The cancer's gone."

Maria, who shared a room with Gloria, has come to understand why her sister needed so much attention.

"You saw how much we loved Gloria, didn't you?" Kristen asked Maria once.

"Yeah," Maria replied.

"We love you as much as we love Gloria," Kristen said. "We love all of you like that. You saw the love in action, so just think about that."

Maria smiled, hugged her mother and released her jealousy.

But it took another loss for the Strausses to realize how far they've come. In October 2008, a little more than a year after Gloria's passing, Doug's father died at age seventy-nine. Doug made sure Steve's life ended with the same holy atmosphere that gave Gloria peace. Then, during the funeral, Doug used a chant from the gregarious former paratrooper's old unit, the 82nd Airborne Division, to provide an emotional send-off.

The soldiers used to say, "Eighty-second Airborne, all the way! Eighty-second Airborne, all the way!" Doug tweaked the chant.

"Eighty-second Airborne, all the way—to heaven!" he exclaimed. "Eighty-second Airborne, all the way—to heaven!"

Doug remembers his eulogy and grins.

"I learned a lot from Gloria, didn't I?" he says.

* * *

Beyond the Strausses, it's been amazing to see how committed their friends have remained. They still hold prayer sessions. They join the Strausses for all of Gloria's remembrances—birthday, funeral, the day she fell into the coma, the day she died. They will never forget Gloria.

The Funai family, who prayed with Gloria and kept her hair stylish, switched religious disciplines, from Presbyterian to Catholic, because of her. They were received into the Catholic Church in time for Easter 2008.

And there have been more encounters with glitter. In fact, they've become so frequent that the Strauss children automatically relate glitter to Gloria.

In spring 2008, about six months after Gloria's death, her good friend, Aleah, sang in the school choir and saw Gloria's face glistening on the plastic cover of her song book. Joy paralyzed her at first. Sunlight streamed through St. Philomena parish's stained glass windows, where students were celebrating a Friday morning Mass, and out of nowhere, out of heaven, their deceased classmate joined them.

Aleah elbowed the girl sitting next to her.

"Can you see that?" she asked.

"No," the girl replied.

Aleah fixated on the image some more, sang some more, and then it faded. After Mass, she sprinted toward her mother.

"Mom, I saw Gloria on my songbook!" she exclaimed.

Mary Ruth calmed her daughter and received the full explanation. Kristen happened to be at Mass that morning, so they scurried over to share the excitement.

Kristen listened to every soul-stirring detail until her eyes welled with tears. She had one request: "Aleah, show me exactly where you were sitting."

Aleah escorted the two women to the precise spot. She stood and pointed. Kristen saw something shining. Aleah bent down to look at the particle.

It was pink glitter.

Only Gloria.

With the songbook tucked under her arm, Aleah picked up the glitter. Then, as she began to walk, another single speck of glitter fell out of her book and landed on her shoe. She cooed. The women smiled.

Only Gloria.

*   *   *

Not all of the Strausses' friends were feeling Gloria's warmth, however. Jen Vertetis was struggling. Her strength yielded to the grief. Shortly after the funeral, she became pregnant with her third child, but the Vertetis family was about to be tested like never before.

Peter, Jen's oldest child, battled problems with his heart and teeth. He went through medication withdrawals and skin infections. And he was having behavioral issues, his aggression rising to troubling levels. Because of his problems, Peter was frequently sent home early from school.

He threw tantrums that left his mother with bruises and bite marks. Jen feared her son would inadvertently harm the unborn child, and her concerns about injury gave way to fears that the new baby would be autistic.

Jen was sick from the pregnancy and sick of hardships. She felt she was failing as a mother, a wife and a friend. She argued often with her husband, Tom—a byproduct of their grief.

One afternoon, she realized she had lost all her faith—in God, in herself—and she trudged through the day with an overwhelming sense of hopelessness. Her shockingly impressive composure had vanished. She couldn't relegate her pain to the fringes of her heart and function as the reliable Jennifer McCann Vertetis whom everyone expected. She was vulnerable, after all.

While driving on the freeway with Peter that day, a semi came inches from smashing her car. In that moment, Jen was sad the truck did not crush them. She just wanted the pain to stop.

After she returned home, she succumbed to tears and cried and cried and cried, the pent-up depression rushing down her face. Then her doorbell rang.

It was Doug and Bob with a bouquet of flowers. They told her that, while praying together at the office, they both saw visions of Gloria looking down at Jen's house and telling them to help her. At that moment, Jen returned to being Jen. She had always been skeptical when others claimed their God moments, even throughout Gloria's holy journey, but now she understood.

"I saw that God was there," she recalled. "He was looking out for me, and Gloria has shown this to me. I knew I had so much to be thankful for, and I just needed to take the time to praise God for all he has given me in my life and not focus on the difficult. It was a turning point in my life.

I don't know how I would have resurfaced from that depression if Gloria had not reached down from Heaven and embraced me."

Several months later, on July 4, 2008, Tom and Jen celebrated the birth of their third child. They named him Glorian. Glorian Gabriel Vertetis.

One day, he will ask about his namesake. He will learn of the beautiful girl who inspired it, how she lifted Mommy from despair and changed the lives of many. He will know her the same as those who lived with her—as an angel—singing and dancing and performing, a star of hope forever gleaming.

The first Strauss family portrait taken after Gloria died. Left to right: Joe, Sam, Doug, Maria, Vincent, Kristen, Anthony and Alissa. © Paul Dudley

ACKNOWLEDGMENTS

I never read the acknowledgments page of any book until I had to write one myself. I used to wonder why a writer would waste so much space just to say thank you, especially in this age of social networking Web sites and instant electronic communication. Is it not easier just to text "THX" these days?

Fortunately, I get it now. It's about the public recognition and the permanence of the gratitude. Nothing says gracias quite like inviting others to join you in the Library of Congress. After the exhausting, emotional process of writing this book, I'm grateful for the opportunity to be grateful.

Thanks to my love, Karen Gaudette, for her patience, for her encouragement and, most important, for her heart. The life we have established together is my reason for rising each morning. Thanks to my parents, Rod and Pam Hightower, for being good listeners and for raising me so well. Thanks to my entire family for being equally supportive, particularly my brother, Kyle Hightower, and both sets of grandparents—Lim and Addie Brewer, and the Reverend James and Barbara Hightower.

Thanks to Mike McCloskey and San Juan Publishing for believing in this project. Thanks to my editor, Holly Wyrwich, for her mastery of the English language. (Great Holly story: She was on a plane editing a chapter once, and a passenger asked her what she reads for fun. She replied, "Editing *is* fun." I think the woman could find a comma splice in a haystack. And she understands the big picture, too.)

Thanks to *The Seattle Times* for trusting me. Frank Blethen, David Boardman, Suki Dardarian, Cathy Henkel, Don Shelton, Bill Reader, Laura Gordon, Mike Stanton—they're among the many newspaper folks who allowed Gloria to become a star.

Thanks to Steve Ringman, for being my sidekick and my confidant, not to mention the ideal photographer for this project.

So many of the Strausses' friends helped turn a difficult experience into a positive one. I could fill another book with their names, but I must highlight a few: Jennifer Vertetis (and family), Lori Rosellini (and family), Mike and Laura Prato, Tom and Kari Curran, Jack and Mary McCann, Kari Mannikko, Kim Freyberg (and family), Mary Ruth (and family), Greg Carras (and family), Stephanie Squires, Sandy Smith, Paul Dudley, Jessica Morley (and family), Theresa Brennan (and family), Kelley Masterson (and family), the Funais, the Turners, the Fantozzis, the D'Angelos, the Caldwells, the Buehrings and the Genzales. Thanks to the faculty and staff at St. Philomena Catholic School and Kennedy High School for treating me like they do their alums. Thanks to the church communities from St. Vincent de Paul and St. Theresa in Federal Way.

Children's Hospital deserves immense credit and a huge thanks for allowing me to follow Gloria so closely during her final days. A saying I learned as a child best describes how I feel: *People don't have to be kind, and if they're kind, they don't have to be kind to you.* We disagreed at times, but I appreciate the cooperative spirit and professionalism the hospital exhibited, and I'm lucky to have witnessed the heartfelt care that Gloria's caretakers gave her daily. And Dr. Julie Park, often in an impossible situation with dying children, should be lauded for her dedication to solve neuroblastoma, the torturous disease that took Gloria from us.

Thanks to Diane Strauss for becoming my mother. Thanks to Pat and Vicki Trimberger and the entire South Bend, Indiana, crew for being so welcoming. Thanks to all the Strausses, Trimbergers and Millers who made me an extension of their families.

Finally, the most important thanks goes to Doug, Kristen, Alissa, Gloria, Maria, Joseph, Anthony, Samuel and Viiiii-ince-ent for their remarkable display of faith and for having the courage to tell their family story during a distressing time. Doug can be my ugly brother for the rest of our lives. Kristen is the sweetest, most genuine person I've ever met. It's no wonder that they've produced seven tender-hearted children, including one whose legacy will reign.

I hope this book has been one long acknowledgment of Gloria's amazing life.

ABOUT THE AUTHOR

Jerry Brewer © Rod Mar

J erry Brewer is a sports columnist for *The Seattle Times*. He was nominated for a 2008 Pulitzer Prize for the "A Prayer for Gloria" series that led to this book. Before coming to Seattle in 2006, Brewer worked at three other newspapers: *The Courier-Journal* in Louisville, Kentucky, *The Orlando Sentinel*, and *The Philadelphia Inquirer*. He has received awards for his work from numerous journalism organizations, including the American Association of Sunday and Features Editors, Associated Press Sports Editors, Society of Professional Journalists, Best of the West, and National Sportscasters and Sportswriters Association. This is his first book.

ABOUT THE PHOTOGRAPHER

Steve Ringman © Jim Bates

Steve Ringman, a native of Mount Vernon, Washington, has photo-graphed the Contra War in Nicaragua; earthquakes in El Salvador and San Francisco; adoption of orphaned children in China; the culture of baseball in Japan and two World Series in the U.S.; global warming in the Arctic and the Bering Sea; and, most recently, malaria-relief efforts in Tanzania and Zambia. In 1982, he photographed one of the earliest series about HIV/AIDS, working with writer Randy Shilts. Ringman was twice named Newspaper Photographer of the Year by the National Press Photographers Association, in 1983 and 1985. A graduate of Brooks Institute of Photography, he has worked for the *San Francisco Chronicle*, *Antioch Daily Ledger* (California), and *Pittsburg Post-Dispatch* (California) before joining *The Seattle Times*.

ABOUT GLORIA'S ANGELS

Gloria's Angels seeks to lift burdens and build communities so people can focus on caring for a family member with a life-threatening condition. The non-profit organization accomplishes its mission in the following ways:

- *Lifting burdens:* guiding families through the maze of services so they can focus on care, not burdensome procedures.
- *Comprehensive approach:* walking with people across the spectrum of needs, partnering with service agencies across all elements of care (medical, spiritual, professional, domestic, community).
- *Filling gaps:* providing for essential needs not covered by other agencies.
- *Building communities:* connecting community-based volunteers with people in their own neighborhood during their times of great need and beyond.

For more information, visit www.gloriasangels.org.

* * *

ALSO AVAILABLE FROM SAN JUAN PUBLISHING

The Light on the Island by Helene Glidden
Once Upon an Island by David Conover
Andrew Henry's Meadow by Doris Burn
Springer's Journey by Naomi Black and Virginia Heaven
True Coaching by Tom Doyle
The Sport Parent's Manual by Tom Doyle

SAN JUAN PUBLISHING
P.O. Box 923
Woodinville, WA 98072
425-485-2813
sanjuanbooks@yahoo.com
www.sanjuanbooks.com

During her first birthday party, Gloria dives into her birthday cake.
Photo courtesy of the Strauss family

Gloria's whimsical sense of humor endeared her to everyone. © Paul Dudley

Opposite page: Lexie Rosellini, Aleah Ruth, and Gloria often hung out together because their families shared a long, loving history. *Above right: Lexie and Gloria at a soccer game.* *Below right: Gloria and Aleah before class at St. Philomena Catholic School.* Photos courtesy of the Strauss family

Gloria and her parents stand in front of the Rosary Basilica during a 2005 pilgrimage to Lourdes, France. Inset: Gloria smiles for the camera while wearing a souvenir from France, her hot pink beret.
Photos courtesy of the Strauss family

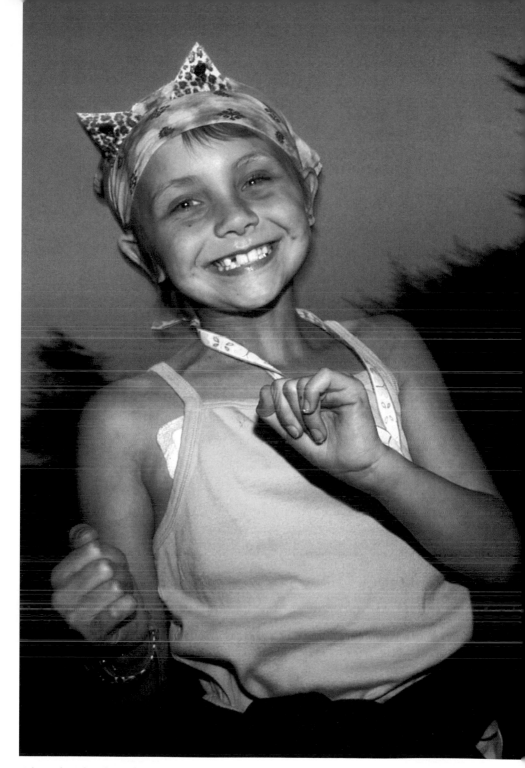

Gloria lost her hair due to chemotherapy treatments, but she managed to hold on to her joyous nature. © Paul Dudley

Together with friend Danielle Brunner, Gloria celebrates her First Communion at age eight. After chemotherapy, Gloria's hair grew back brown before returning to its blond color. Photo courtesy of the Strauss family

During a May 2007 prayer session at their home, Kristen and Doug lay hands on a resting Gloria. This scene was typical of nights at the Strauss house. © Steve Ringman, *The Seattle Times*

Opposite page: Gloria holds onto Vincent as Anthony pushes her around. When she was first given a wheelchair in June 2007, Gloria used it more as a toy to entertain her brothers. © Steve Ringman, *The Seattle Times*

Following pages: Kristen opens her Bible to Matthew 10:1, which includes scripture about healing that her Grandma Miller had underlined years ago. Kristen took the highlighted passage as a sign from God.
© Steve Ringman, *The Seattle Times*

Mission of the Twelve. 3,
his tour of all the tow
taught in their synagog
the good news of God's
every sickness and diseas
of the crowds, his heart
pity. They were lying pros
tion, like sheep without a
said to his disciples: "The
but laborers are scarce. 38
master to send out labore
harvest."

CHAPTER 10

1 Then he summoned his t
and gave them authority to
spirits and to cure sickness a
every kind.

2* The names of the twelv
these: first Simon, now known
his brother Andrew; James, Zc
d his brother John; 3 Philip ar
Thomas and Matthew the t
son of Alphaeus, and
the Zealot Party member
, who betrayed him. 5 Jesu
n mission as the Twelve, a
the following instructions:
o not visit pagan territory ar
a Samaritan town, 6* Go ins
lost sheep of the house of Isra

35: Lk 8, 1.
36: Jer 50, 6; Ez 34,
5; Mk 6, 34.
37f: Lk 10, 2; Jn 4, 35.
10, 2-5: Mk 3, 16-19; Lk 6,
13-16; Acts 1, 13.
6: 15, 24.
7: 3, 2; 4, 17.
9: Mk 6, 8f; Lk 9, 3.
10, 4.
10: Lk 10, 7; 1 Cor 9,
14; 3 Jn 8.
11-15: Mk 6, 10f; Lk 9, 4f.
10, 5-12.
14: Acts 13, 51; 18, 6.
15: 11, 24; Jude 7.

16: Lk 10, 3
20.
17-22: Mk 13, 9-
12-19; Jn
17: Acts 5, 40
18: Jn 15, 27
19: Ex 4, 11
6-10; Lk 1,
21f: 24, 9.13
24f: Lk 6, 40; Jn
15, 20.
26-33: Lk 12, 2-9
26: Mk 4, 22; Lk
1 Tm 5, 25
28: 1 Pt 1, 7; P
10

9, 35—10, 1: Having preached and ministered wide
Galilee, Jesus sees the people's need for prophetic leader
cf Nm 27, 17. He therefore expands his missionary ac
by conferring his own powers on certain of his disc
10, 2-33: These verses, which conserve Jesus' instr
to his disciples for their missionary activity, constitute a m
for all Christian missioners. Certain of his prophecie
incorporated into the discourse because they reflected
church's experience (10, 17-21); cf 2 Cor 11, 23ff; Acts
40; 24, 1-23.
10, 12f: The blessing referred to is a wish
blessing, once invoked, is consid
n undeserving house
urns and

Jesus continued
and villages. He
, he proclaimed
n, and he cured
36* At the sight
as moved with
e from exhaus-
pherd. 37* He
rvest is good
g the harvest
o gather his

ve disciples
el unclean
disease of

ostles are
eter, and
ee's son,
artholo-
ollector;
ldaeus;
l Judas
t these
giving

o not
after
* As

14.
1.
*

you go, make this announcement: 'The reign of God is at hand!' 8 Cure the sick, raise the dead, heal the leprous, expel demons. The gift you have received, give as a gift. 9* Provide yourselves with neither gold nor silver nor copper in your belts; 10* no traveling bag, no change of shirt, no sandals, no walking staff. The workman, after all, is worth his keep.

11* "Look for a worthy person in every town or village you come to and stay with him until you leave. 12† As you enter his home bless it. 13 If the home is deserving, your blessing will descend on it. If it is not, your blessing will return to you. 14* If anyone does not receive you or listen to what you have to say, leave that house or town, and once outside it shake its dust from your feet. 15* I assure you, it will go easier for the region of Sodom and Gomorrah on the day of judgment than it will for that town.

16* "What I am doing is sending you out like sheep among wolves. You must be clever as snakes and innocent as doves. 17* Be on your guard with respect to others. They will hale you into court, they will flog you in their synagogues. 18* You will be brought to trial before rulers and kings, to give witness before them and before the Gentiles on my account. 19* When they hand you over, do not worry about what you will say or how you will say it. When the hour comes, you will be given what you are to say. 20 You yourselves will not be the speakers; the Spirit of your Father will be speaking in you. 21* "Brother will hand over brother to death, and the father his child; children will turn against parents and have them put to death. 22 You will be hated by all on account of me. But whoever holds out till the end will escape death. 23† When they persecute you in one town, flee to the next. I solemnly assure you, you will not have covered the towns of Israel before the Son of Man comes.

24* "No pupil outranks his teacher, no slave his master. 25 The pupil should be glad to become like his teacher, the slave like his master. If they call the head of . . . house Beelzebul, how . . . embers of . . .

MARK
LUKE
JOHN
ACTS
PHIL
COL
1TH
2TH
1TI
2TI
TITU
PHIN
HEBR
JAMS
1PET

Father Jim Northrop leads an evening Mass on the Strausses' deck in July 2007 to thank God for helping Gloria when she was able to walk again after more than a week of crippling pain. © Steve Ringman, *The Seattle Times*

Opposite page: Gloria listens intently to Father Jim's message, showing the reverence she always had for priests and other authority figures. © Steve Ringman, *The Seattle Times*

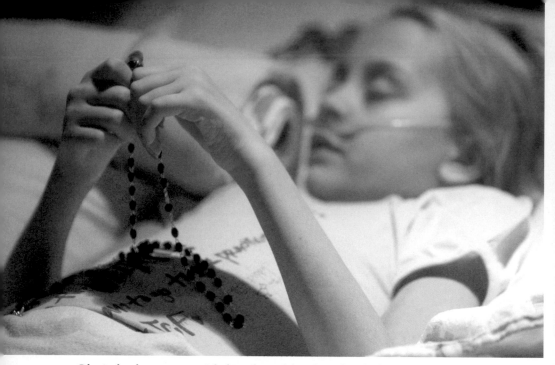

Gloria leads a rosary with friends and family at her bedside at Seattle Children's Hospital. © Steve Ringman, *The Seattle Times*

Gloria looks up as Jessica Morley tells her: "I want you to know I'm never giving up on this miracle. I love you." © Steve Ringman, *The Seattle Times*

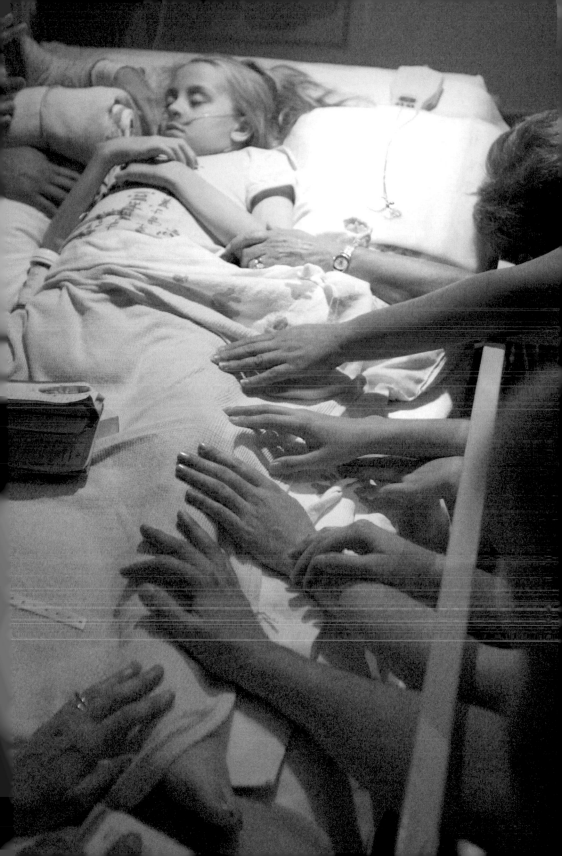

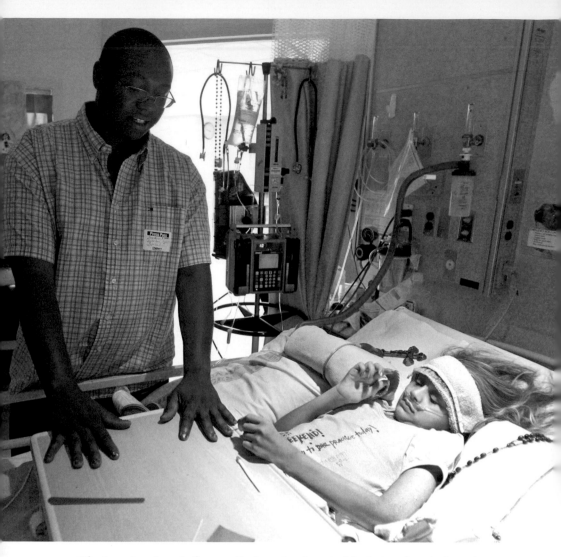

Gloria paints Jerry's fingernails from her hospital bed nine days before she died. She colored them pink and glued rhinestones on top and asked that he keep them painted for at least a day. © Steve Ringman, *The Seattle Times*

Previous page: On September 12, 2007, Gloria started a prayer session by asking God to heal her and others in the most eloquent manner she had ever spoken. Then she rested her eyes and let her prayer warriors do the rest. © Steve Ringman, *The Seattle Times*

Joe rubs Gloria's head with the rest of the Strausses nearby at a wake on September 26, 2007, in the Kennedy High School chapel.
© Steve Ringman, *The Seattle Times*

Following page: Anthony holds his sister's photo high as he rides on the shoulders of family friend Andrew Barfoot at the funeral procession on September 27. More than 2,000 relatives, friends, students and strangers came to say goodbye to Gloria at the Kennedy High gym.
© Steve Ringman, *The Seattle Times*